Anger

For over a decade, The New York Public Library and Oxford University Press have annually invited a prominent figure in the arts and letters to give a series of lectures on a topic of his or her choice. Subsequently these lectures become the basis of a book jointly published by the Library and the Press. For 2002 and 2003 the two institutions asked seven noted writers, scholars, and critics to offer a "meditation on temptation" on one of the seven deadly sins. *Anger* by Robert A. F. Thurman is the fifth book from this lecture series. Previous books from The New York Public Library/ Oxford University Press Lectures are:

The Old World's New World by C. Vann Woodward

Culture of Complaint: The Fraying of America by Robert Hughes

Witches and Jesuits: Shakespeare's Macbeth by Garry Wills

Visions of the Future: The Distant Past, Yesterday, Today, Tomorrow
by Robert Heilbroner

Doing Documentary Work by Robert Coles

The Sun, the Genome, and the Internet by Freeman J. Dyson

The Look of Architecture by Witold Rybczynski

Visions of Utopia by Edward Rothstein, Herbert Muschamp,
and Martin E. Marty

Also by Robert A. F. Thurman

Infinite Life: Seven Virtues for Living Well

The Tibetan Book of the Dead

Circling the Sacred Mountain: A Spiritual Adventure Through the Himalayas

Inner Revolution: Life, Liberty, and the Pursuit of Real Happiness

Essential Tibetan Buddhism

The Central Philosophy of Tibet

Anger

The Seven Deadly Sins

Robert A. F. Thurman

The New York Public Library

OXFORD
UNIVERSITY PRESS

2005

OXFORD
UNIVERSITY PRESS

Oxford   New York
Auckland Bangkok Buenos Aires Cape Town Chennai
Dar es Salaam Delhi Hong Kong Istanbul Karachi Kolkata
Kuala Lumpur Madrid Melbourne Mexico City Mumbai Nairobi
São Paulo Shanghai Taipei Tokyo Toronto

Published by Oxford University Press, Inc.
198 Madison Avenue, New York, New York, 10016
www.oup.com

Library of Congress Cataloging-in-Publication Data
Thurman, Robert A. F.
  Anger : the seven deadly sins / Robert A. F. Thurman.
    p. cm.
  Includes bibliographical and index.
  ISBN 0-19-516975-1
 1. Anger—Religious aspects—Buddhism.
 2. Patience—Religious aspects—Buddhism.
 3. Religious life—Buddhism.
 I. Title.
BQ4430.A53T489 2004
294.3'5698—dc22   2004012549

All artwork appears courtesy of Tibet House U. S.

Book design by planettheo.com

9 8 7 6 5 4 3 2 1
Printed in the United States of America
on acid-free paper

Experiences are preceded by mind, led by mind, produced by mind. If one speaks or acts with an impure mind, suffering follows, even as the cart-wheel follows the hoof of the ox.

Experiences are preceded by mind, led by mind, produced by mind. If one speaks or acts with a pure mind, happiness follows, like a shadow that never departs.

Those who entertain such thoughts as "He abused me, he beat me, he defeated me, he robbed me," will not calm their anger.

Those who do not entertain such thoughts as "He abused me, he beat me, he defeated me, he robbed me," will calm their anger.

Here in the world, anger is never pacified by anger. It is pacified by love. This is the eternal truth.

Some do not realize that we are all heading for death. Those who do realize it will compose their quarrels.

Happy indeed we live, friendly amid the haters. Among men who hate we dwell free from hate.

Let one give up anger, renounce conceit, and overcome all fetters. Suffering does not befall him who is unattached to words and things and is free of possessions.

I call him a charioteer who holds back the arisen anger as though holding back a swerving chariot. Others are only holders of reins.

Dhammapada, The Way of Truth, I, 1–6; XV, 1; XVII, 1–2.
Sangharakshita translation (slightly modified)

Contents

Editor's Note

This volume is part of a lecture and book series on the Seven Deadly Sins cosponsored by The New York Public Library and Oxford University Press. Our purpose was to invite scholars and writers to chart the ways we have approached and understood evil, one deadly sin at a time. Through both historical and contemporary explorations, each writer finds the conceptual and practical challenges that a deadly sin poses to spirituality, ethics, and everyday life.

The notion of the Seven Deadly Sins did not originate in the Bible. Sources identify early lists of transgressions classified in the fourth century by Evagrius of Pontus and then by John of Cassius. In the sixth century, Gregory the Great formulated the traditional seven. The sins were ranked by increasing severity, and judged to be the greatest offenses to the soul and the root of all other sins. As certain sins were subsumed into others and similar terms were used interchangeably according to theological review, the list evolved to include the seven as we know them: Pride, Greed, Lust, Envy, Gluttony, Anger, and Sloth. To counter these violations, Christian theologians classified the Seven Heavenly Virtues—the cardinal: Prudence, Temperance, Justice, Fortitude, and the theological: Faith, Hope, and Charity. The sins inspired medieval and

Renaissance writers including Chaucer, Dante, and Spenser, who personified the seven in rich and memorable characters. Depictions grew to include associated colors, animals, and punishments in hell for the deadly offenses. Through history, the famous list has emerged in theological and philosophical tracts, psychology, politics, social criticism, popular culture, and art and literature. Whether the deadly seven to you represent the most common human foibles or more serious spiritual shortcomings, they stir the imagination and evoke the inevitable question—what is *your* deadly sin?

Our contemporary fascination with these age-old sins, our struggle against or celebration of them, reveals as much about our continued desire to define human nature as it does about our divine aspirations. I hope that this book and its companions invite the reader to indulge in a similar reflection on vice, virtue, the spiritual, and the human.

Elda Rotor

Anger

Preamble

I am angry at anger—I hate it. I want to get rid of it. I want to be free from it. I want it never again to take me over and use my body, speech, and mind to harm myself and others. But hating it puts me into a double-bind—if I get furious with anger, it does take me over. To stop anger, I can't be angry. If I stop being angry, no matter what, I attain the goal. But if I'm not angry with anger, will I after all get back into it?

I have always had a problem with anger. I used to lose my temper very quickly, intensely, and it would sweep me away into a fierce swirl of thoughts, sudden words, sometimes a furious movement, long ago perhaps a charge, a blow, a hurling. Was I born with this hot temper? Did it come from early childhood experience? I do remember having to defend myself against my older brother, my face flashing bright red as I breathlessly channeled the fear surging up inside back outward in a wild rage aiming to make him fear me instead. Was there an element of playacting at work in that? Sometimes. Did I really lose it? Sometimes. There was a fine line.

I had several disadvantages in these struggles, one of them quite big, as it seemed at the time. Until the age of twelve I was smaller; his reach let him hit me before I could hit him back. Even worse, I seemed to have a phobia about hitting a face, any face. No matter how furious, when my fist swung toward a human face, it swerved away as if magnetically repelled and struck the shoulder. This phobia was so bad I couldn't box in school, and I had to take up fencing. I disliked slashing and being slashed in saber practice, so I stuck to the foil. No problem in sticking the rubber-tipped flexible épée into the padded belly or chest of my opponent.

My hot temper made me quite sharp of tongue. Until sprouting up at twelve, I was the small guy with the big mouth, clever enough to find someone's weak spot and needle it. Often I would go too far, and there would be larger trouble. Luckily, when cool I had a good sense of humor and made friends easily, and so enjoyed a wide circle. As I grew and developed intellectually, I was quite fierce as a debater, and certainly seem to have been too intimidating as a college student, grad student, and younger teacher. When I was a Tibetan Buddhist monk, my old Mongolian "root Lama," primary spiritual teacher, actually prohibited me from learning the special techniques and tricks of Tibetan formal debate, saying that I was able to debate quite well without knowing them and, if I did have all the tricks at my command, I "would make too many people unhappy"! I was quite frustrated at this but accepted it after some complaint, and no doubt numbers of colleagues since would be grateful if they had known who had spared them what.

In my birth family, as the middle son, I was a peacemaker among my parents, grandparents, and brothers, all being highly emotional and even theatrical in their histrionic rows. Yet later, when I resigned my monastic vows, reentered the world, married, and did the work of being husband to my wife and father to my children, I discovered still lurking deep down in my habitual patterns the impatience, frustration, and, yes, hot anger that must have come down through my paternal lineage of southern rednecks. I tried to restrain the more obnoxious of these male and patriarchal dominance feelings and behaviors, using the philosophical, psychological, contemplative, and "mind-reform" insights and techniques that I had learned as a monk, with varying degrees of success in different situations. I am still imperfect in my patience and self-restraint, though I have experienced enough improvement to feel grateful to the tradition I am still learning, and to feel confident intellectually that the insights are sound and the methods effective.

The most important work of our generations for our world is to use a new level of introspective insight and self-mastery to break the chain of descent of inherited personal, family, and cultural violence of mind, speech, and body. We cannot bring into this world that real peace so urgently needed by future generations without freeing ourselves from bondage to our inherited anger and its violence. We cannot accept the conventional wisdom that calls this impossible, idealistic, utopian, since a world of Mutual Assured Destruction will assuredly destroy itself. Besides, all prophets and visionaries of all times have concurred in foreseeing a new heaven and a new earth, rather than the end of all life. Finally, even if the worst should happen, it is our duty to do everything in our power to bring about the best, so that we will have no regret, no matter what.

There are two extreme views of anger that I will take as the poles between which I hope to expound a middle way in this essay. I call them resignation to anger and resignation from anger.

The first extreme view is that there is nothing you can do about anger, except perhaps modulate it a little bit. There are both religious and secular versions of this view. The religious version claims that "God" is an angry God, even Jesus is hot-tempered when he kicks over the money changers' tables and criticizes Pharisees and others. Anger is God-given. We all are angry. Anger is healthy. We need anger to right wrongs, overturn social evils, revolt against oppression. Anger is only deadly, sinful, or bad when it is unfair, excessive, or self-destructive. Anyone who tries to control or overcome anger is delusional, trying to be perfect, in the grip of Lucifer.

The secular version of this view argues from a social Darwinist version of biology, that we are all "hardwired" with anger. We need it to protect ourselves from danger of aggression or oppression. It is our source of courage in a fight. Anyone who thinks we can get rid of it has never read Freud or his successors.

The second extreme view is that anger can be totally eradicated. It absolutely is a deadly sin. It is completely destructive, unjustified in any circumstance. We must manage it out of existence. We must learn to meditate, to transcend all emotionality. It is a fire and can only burn us. When we quench that fire, we have attained Nirvana, Godliness, perfection. We must all become saints and can somehow become ultimately perfect, superhuman.

The first extreme view is predominant in the West, in both religious and secular versions, and is also strongly represented in the East. The second extreme view is present in the West in the forms of Gnosticism and most kinds of Judaic, Christian, and Islamic mysticisms, and more widespread in the East in the forms of dualistic Buddhism and Hindu and Taoist mysticisms. So the East-West division is not really very useful, nor the monotheist-nontheist division, nor the Christian-Buddhist division. The middle way I will elaborate here is more complex than these stereotyped polarities suggest.

To make things even more complex, just for fun, I both agree and disagree with each of these extreme positions, the resignation to anger and the resignation from anger.

In regard to the first extreme position, resignation to anger, I agree in the sense that anger has an energy that cannot be avoided altogether. It is like fire, and fire is elemental. It burns and can be painful. It is unrealistic to think that fire can be eliminated from a world it constitutes, keeping the cooler aspects of that world intact. On the other hand, I disagree in the sense that the fire analogy doesn't mean that anger is fire, nothing else, and that there is no fire without anger. The angry God in ancient myths is a tribal projection, not an ultimate reality. "He" is a tribal god among tribal gods, no more or less angry than the ordinary people of that tribe. Jesus was depicted as angry by angry writers of the Gospels, early Jewish Christians who were using his story to portray their enemies, the Rabbinic Jews who would not accept Jesus as the messiah, as evil. Freud was a good observer of human nature, but he was only a beginner in a young science of psychology in a violent culture, which was relatively backward in what the Indians long ago called the "Inner Science" of psychology. It is a tenet central to the patriarchal, militaristic cultures of our recent historic record of the last five or so millennia that anger cannot be avoided—therefore we must have professional armies, police, prisons, rigid social controls, and capital punishment. But we can do better. No need to give up.

In regard to the second extreme position, resignation from anger, I also both agree and disagree. I agree that anger is inevitably destructive, never justified or useful. I do agree that by cultivating critical wisdom and stabilized concentration to the highest degree, it is possible to withdraw so completely from conventional, over-substantialized, illusory reality that the fire of anger, the flood of passion, the cage of delusion—all can be eliminated utterly, and the supreme bliss of Nirvana can be attained permanently and completely. There is nothing evil or unrealistic about this. Nirvana is supreme goodness, is the very heart of "God," as discerned by many a saint, West as well as East, and a more sophisticated Inner Science of psychology is in the process of discovering that again in the West.

But I disagree with resignation from anger when turning to the question of what is Nirvana? What is it for? Is it just for one's own isolated peace? Are there not still other beings in the world? Will your Nirvana destroy the world of pain of the other beings? Is "God" all heart, disembodied, neglectful of illusory-but-still-imprisoned beings? Is there not a good use for fire, no longer bound up with anger, to warm, to illuminate, to burn away the suffering of others? Can wisdom not wield fire, hold it up as lamplight, to illuminate the darkness of ignorance, prejudice, and self-centered misknowledge? Isn't Buddha fiercely intolerant of the doom for others of endless suffering? Does he not manifest embodiments of fierceness, just as God does? Do not saints return to care for the nonsaintly?

Anger when bound up with hate overwhelms the reasonable person with a painful vice-grip and uses him or her as a slave or tool to injure or destroy the target of that hateful anger, regardless of whether this action destroys the tool in the process. It is never useful, never justifiable, always harmful to self as well as others. When organized systematically, it turns into all-out war, it becomes nuclear fission. But fortunately it can always be controlled, restrained, and ultimately prevented, avoided, and transcended. The slave of anger can definitely free him- or herself. No need to resign to its dominion. Then, the raw, neutral energy of anger, the searing flame of fury, the power of the "peaceful atom," can itself become a power tool. It can warm the house, light the darkness, burn away the bonds of ignorance. Compassion can use this fire with fierce effectiveness to destroy the suffering of other beings. Anger usually monopolizes fire, turning it to destructive ends. Our goal surely is to conquer anger, but not to destroy the fire it has misappropriated. We will wield that fire with wisdom and turn it to creative ends.

Now here comes the most challenging statement for us materialists, which, if true, turns our whole "scientific" worldview inside out, upside down, and opposite reversed. The ultimate fire in our relative reality, the pulsar, supernova flame, the doomsday fire that split atoms long before Einstein and nuclear reactors, turns out after all to be *the mind on fire, the searing flame of critical wisdom*, an ultimate energy harnessed and released by the mind. And this fact, long known by buddhas, can be proven true in our personal experience! Wisdom is *prajnya*, superknowledge, the superintelligence of buddhas, the critical insight that fully analyzes both the superficial appearances and the ultimate natures of things in the adamantine drive to discover their true reality. Taking things apart analytically does destroy them in some sense, dissects them, sees through them, confronts their ultimate nonexistence—in order to discern precisely the real qualities of their relative existence. Once such discovery and discernment is complete, one is freed from being the tool and becomes the master of those very deepest energies. Only then can one direct the fierce energy, formerly imprisoned by frantic anger, to reshape the world of things, the better to sustain the lives and liberations of sensitive beings.

Therefore, the Buddhist "infinitheistic," scientific, psychological tradition symbolizes the liberating, transcendent wisdom as a sharp sword with brilliant flames blazing from its tip: a dissective scalpel, a brilliant lamp, a blazing metal cutter. Monotheistic traditions discern through faith this ultimate intelligence and energy as the "mind of God," and see it as able to create and to destroy every thing and every being. The difference between the infinitheists and the monotheists is that the latter rule out human access to this ultimate enlightened mind, rule out the evolutionary possibility for humans and other beings to attain perfect buddha-hood for themselves. Therefore, they rule out the evolutionary possibility for the human being to attain total freedom from anger. Beyond that, they cannot imagine that the enlightened human can wield the fire formerly controlled by anger to destroy the world of ignorance and then create a world of liberation for all others. Most monotheists that is, since a few mystics and gnostics here and there have experienced the "mind of God." But we hardly ever get to know them, since our authoritarian Western societies tend to eliminate them as soon as they arise!

Critical wisdom's transformation of the energy of anger into the power of compassion turns the conventional world of egocentric beings inside out—because the subtle mind turns out to be more powerful than any gross matter, upside down—because the highest power of God, the incandescent flames of star-destroying supernovas, turns out to be in their own minds, their responsibility, and opposite reverse—because others become more important than oneself, wisdom becomes more blissful than ignorance, freedom more natural than attachment, and love more powerful than hateful anger. This is where the complete conquest of anger becomes possible—living in the truth, essential for survival—living free of fear, essential for "supervival"—and living in bliss, thriving, and blessing others!

CHAPTER ONE

The Momentous Present

It is entirely good that we should spend some time together meditating on the dreaded terror of anger. It has long been understood as a "deadly sin" in the Christian and Islamic West. In the Buddhist East, anger (*dvesha*) is called an addiction (*klesha*), or a poison (*visha*), one of the three root poisons (along with greed and delusion) that constitute the real cause of the life of suffering, the *samsara*, or endless life cycle of unenlightened frustration.

It is especially important to meditate together on anger, as painful a subject as it may be, because our nation and the world stand on the brink of another major outburst of war. "War" is but the name for "organized anger." Culturally organized anger sets the standard for our militaristic, violent lifestyle, modeled by heroes from Achilles to the Terminator. Politically organized anger has now become America's aggressive (hiding under the cloak of "preemptive") world war to conquer "terror" that we are being misled into by our corporatized government and its media propaganda. This looming world war is openly called "World War IV" by a former head of the CIA (counting the "Cold War" as World War III). It represents a major escalation of the planetary war system that has been growing uninterruptedly for over a century.

All along we have thought we were coming to the end of war. Woodrow Wilson thought World War I would end all wars. In the 1990s some thought the end of the Cold War was the end of history. We were standing in a light of hope at the dawn of a new century in which a peaceful global society was just beginning to seem possible. Suddenly an election was subverted (as seemed obvious to almost everyone on the planet except ourselves), any kind of postwar, "peace dividend" was lost, the 9/11 disaster brought the biblical "Tower of Babel" catastrophe to life in our mass unconscious, and now we are deeply submerged in an "endless war on terror." We are once again enslaved by the economy, culture, and ideology of endless war.

Anger channels energy into war. Thermonuclear anger, chemical anger, biological anger become weapons of mass destruction and clearly can destroy all life on this small planet (though from the commonsense continuity-of-life perspective not a single being is guaranteed sweet oblivion, just loss of present life-form and home planet, leaving continuing terrified beings to find new homes in which to suffer). The potentially endless world war deifies the forms of anger, that dominate the world system more than ever and support its violent economies, that its arts and cultures, its media, its educational curricula, its authoritarian community and family patterns, and its individual personality constellations.

It thus becomes all the more urgent that we examine anger, look at its nature, evaluate whether it is indeed a sin or a poison, decide just how "deadly" it is. The key question: Is anger merely an inevitable part of life and so must be borne and managed with resignation? Or can it be confronted and overcome in this life, hence not be tolerated but opposed and defeated, individually, socially, even globally?

CHAPTER TWO

Resigning to Anger —A Brief Survey

How does anger emerge as a "deadly sin" in the West? Anger was considered "deadly" or "mortal" among sins because it is lethal to the soul's life in God, fatal to our connection to the divine bliss. If you die holding anger in your heart, that is, without repenting it, confessing it, and acting to free yourself from it, you condemn yourself to hellish states of existence. Thus there was nothing "deadly" about anger in the West without the cosmic context of real future existence for persons after death in either heaven or hell. Likewise, anger is also considered "deadly" in the East (though the technical term "mortal" is not used in the same way, anger is symbolized by a poisonous snake), because it causes people in this life to kill each other or kill themselves, and further causes people to take the most wretched rebirths, not only in hell realms but also in ghost (*pretan*) realms, brute animal realms, titan realms, and the most miserable sort of human realms—a much wider set of really horrid biological options!

Many contemporary people still think of anger as "deadly," now considered a "negative emotion," "sin" not being too popular an idea except in fundamentalist or mystical religious circles. The cosmological context of the commonsense prospect of a future existence has faded drastically, and so "deadly" now can only mean "fatal" to chances for happiness in this life, and possibly fatal to this life through killing or being killed. But there is little sense anymore of an emotion or action being "deadly" to the soul, since materialists and merely ideologically religious persons (still culturally materialistic) don't really feel they "have" a "soul," and therefore experience little visceral concern about future rebirth or personal continuity. Some religious pollsters say that nearly 90 percent, or some other preposterously large percentage, of Americans believe there will be a future existence for them and are confident they will go to heaven (either by the grace of Jesus or by calling on God directly if they are Jewish or Muslim). But I find such poll results impossible to believe from my experience of people around town. Even if they were true, the kind of future existence considered probable by such persons does not seem to be one where anger can get you in much trouble. At least it can't get you into a kind of trouble that Jesus or God can't get you out of—so it's not that superdeadly for you. On top of that, God and Jesus both seem to manifest themselves and allow for in others a type of righteous anger against infidels, sinners, and all nonelect persons both below and abroad.

Thus, anger is not really thought of in the contemporary religious West as that serious a problem. It's kind of like a natural phenomenon, like a storm or a bolt of lightning, and perhaps even rather respected as a male prerogative and a privilege of authority. Women's anger is perhaps more frowned on behaviorally, thought of as shrewish and hysterical. Then there is righteous anger, against criminality and injustice, slackers and busybodies, luxury and destitution, which ranges from individuals to be punished to communities against whom there are crusades to be waged. So some contemporary religious persons can strive to restrain anger as somehow morally and practically problematic, but somehow they also respect it, allow lots of uses for it, and consider it ultimately to be beyond full understanding and control, in the province of Nature or God. They love it in the form of capital punishment, draconian prison laws, and crusading wars on drugs, terrorism, illiteracy, and so forth.

Now the secularists, among whom I think are most of the people I know (in spite of supposedly being only a mere 5 to 10 percent of Americans), have a very different view of anger. They relegate the "deadly sin" type of anger to the dustbin of concepts used by religious institutions to suppress the natural human being. They are entirely averse to ideas of sin or guilt in general. They are concerned by recent scientific evidence of the debilitating, health-eroding effects of anger, though they may suspect that such evidence is faulty, coming from bias due to the intrusion of religious thinking into the laboratory. Anyway, these folks are fond of anger and eager to rehabilitate it as a useful emotion or energy by learning the latest techniques of "anger management." Modern liberated women are particularly determined to reclaim their own rightful access to anger, to make use of it to help them throw off male chauvinist intimidation, domination, and oppression. They realize that it can be destructive to self, to relationships, and to others, but they feel that in their situation of long-endured, unrelenting oppression, it operates invisibly, underground, in oppressive economic, cultural, and social relationships, and will inevitably harm them if not brought out into the open and wielded and directed away from themselves. Secularists have no fear of unpleasant future existences, they are determined to improve things here and now, and they see anger as a powerful energy to be employed in that enterprise, eliminating the obstacles to clear and present happiness.

I am much in sympathy with their courage and their aims. But I wonder about the realism of the context within which they make their choices, and whether they are using this energy of anger to the best advantage. One thing that they share with their religious contemporaries is the idea that anger is an inevitable force, a force of nature, something "hardwired" in them and in others—so they do not adopt the goal of overcoming it. They practice restraint in some contexts, of course, as everyone must, but they consider any project to transcend it doomed at the outset. This makes them averse to peacemaking, disarmament, nonviolence in lifestyle; they consider all such attempts to be unrealistic utopianism. There are also still a few remaining revolutionaries, Marxists or Maoists, who glorify anger and righteous violence

Now Western religious people do have codes of ethics, both in the Jewish Bible and in the Christian Gospels. Anger causes the breaking of these codes, causes killing, slander, maliciousness. So, although they think that they will be saved from the consequences of their anger by higher, angrier powers, they do have motive and precept to restrain their anger, moderate it, try not to let it push them into sinful acts. As the Jewish Bible says, in Psalms 4:4, "Be angry, but sin not!" In Matthew 21:22, Jesus says, "But I say to you that everyone who is angry with his brother will be liable to judgment!"

The secularists lose their fear of future hells via their doctrine of annihilation at death. So, they feel more free to challenge authority, are daring in their efforts to right injustice, and tend to be humanistic activists. They also have their human rights codes of ethics about respecting others' lives, property, bodies, and so on, and they know these codes will be broken when under the spell of anger.

But neither of these Western combatants on the field of anger have much chance of winning the battle against their formidable enemy. The religious ones don't try that hard to challenge anger, since they believe that God models anger, has done so from the beginning, and that it would be the sin of pride to think they could alter their own nature. They also think that anger can be good when you are righteous. The humanist ones don't try very hard either, since they think of anger as a good thing, a natural energy for self-preservation, a neurobiological survival-enhancing reaction, and they don't think that unethical actions will have any long-term damaging consequences, since they think they will be utterly annihilated just by dying. So neither of these types considers anger very deadly; thus, neither has a strong likelihood of developing any real control over it.

It is no accident that these two types make up the vast majority of carriers of the modern or postmodern Western and Western-derived culture. This culture is, in fact, the most angry yet, in the sense of most violent and militaristic culture yet apparent on this planet. In spite of our admiration for Athens, we are the Spartans' Spartans, the Romans' Romans, the Imperialists' imperialists. We Americans in particular, still-in-denial heirs of the mass genocides of the Native Americans and the slavery holocaust of the African Americans, children of the Pentagon, wielders of nuclear weapons, producers of chemical and germ warfare agents of unprecedented virulence and quantity—ours is the most militaristic culture ever to manifest on Mother Earth. We spawn mini-militaristic cultures all over the globe, dominated by puppet-like dictators, propped up by militaries manufactured in our image and equipped with our secondhand arms, but never allowed to reach the same massive proportions as us, the inspiring model.

I don't mean to go overboard with the vision of America's imperialistic aspect, recently so extremely prominent since our democracy was compromised. The point here is that anger, its profile, its anchoring habits, its systematic cultivation and channeling into socially internal and militarily international violence, is part of the disciplines taught for membership in our culture. At a young age we watch the cartoons Road Runner and Tom and

Jerry, which relentlessly imprint violence into our nervous systems. At school we are taught the Battle Hymn of the Republic, and we sing our war-glorifying national anthem. We are taught to read and revere the *Iliad*, to admire the battles of David and the Israelites against all manner of enemies, to be awe-inspired by Shakespeare's chronicling of the violent deeds of the English kings as well as those of Caesar. We root for Hamlet to waste his uncle, and in the current cinema we love Rambo, *The Terminator, Star Wars, Alien* fighters, Bruce Lee, *Kill Bill,* and so on. At school we have gymnasiums and stadiums, where we gear up for mini war games such as football, soccer, basketball, hockey, lacrosse, wrestling, and track-and-field competitions, cultivating such battle skills as teamwork, focused anger at the opponent, running, javelin, discus, and so on.

Facing this context of the culture in which we have been brought up and conditioned, not to say brainwashed, we should be alert to a strong resistance within ourselves to the idea that anger is a detriment, that it has negative consequences. Yet we must entertain such an idea and explore it carefully, if we are to free ourselves from individual and collective enslavement to this militaristic culture of anger, violence, and war.

Here we should confront the argument often leveled against the self-critique of Euro-American militaristic culture, namely that "all cultures are the same, China, India, Iran, southeast Asia, not to mention Korea, Mongolia, Japan, and Tibet, all have been and are just as prone to violence, subject to a long history of war and atrocity and slaughter. Why should we feel bad just because we are so good at conquering the world in the modern period, and are still on top at this moment?"

This criticism has some merit, to be sure. When we first turn East, we find epic poems of battles—the Indian *Mahabharata* (ca. fourth century B.C.E.) is thirty-five times longer than the *Iliad* and filled with Achilles-like swashbuckling Rambos like Bhima, Drona, and Arjuna; there is gruesome slaughter, treachery, and woman-abuse as well as wise counsel and stirring tales. We find works of political science with the most Machiavellian strata-gems, such as Kautilya's *Arthashastra* (ca. third century B.C.E.). We find cynicism. We find histories of wars, battles, usurpations, intrigues, assassinations, and so forth. In the *Vedas* (ca. 1500 B.C.E.) of India, we find stirring tribal war songs, evocations of the fierce Father-God Indra, thunderbolt-bearer, also known as Gramaghataka, city-smasher, and calls for victory in battle. In the founding Hindu Scripture, the *Bhagavadgita* (ca. third century C.E.), we listen to a monotheistic God, Vishnu in his incarnation as Krishna, tell the doubtful prince Arjuna he must fight and kill his enemies because it is his religious duty as a king and warrior, and that it is God himself who is ultimately responsible for their deaths, so not to worry. In China, the *Book of Odes* and the *Book of History* (ca. sixth century B.C.E.) recount and celebrate many a battle and warrior. And so for every nation in Asia if we look carefully at their records. Plus ça change!

So we do find in the "East" the same egocentric sense of selfishness, anchored in the same delusion of the substantiality of the self and expressing itself both in the desire to consume the other and the fear and anger against the other's perceived threat to consume one's self. As for god-figures, there are the ancient tribal, highly violent, angry and fearsome forms of the gods, the famous Indra of the *Veda,* who waxes highly wrathful against the enemies of the Vedic peoples, like Iahwe and Zeus and Odin. Then there are the monotheistic forms of Vishnu and Shiva, who can manifest in many ways. The Mahakala "Great Time" form of Vishnu revealed in the *gita* is ultimately terrifying, angry, and destructive, devourer of worlds and the Bhairava ("Terrifier") form of Shiva who dances the destruction of universes—both are exquisitely destructive and powerfully model anger. Then there are the Durga and Kali forms of the Great Mother Goddess, who is angry and violent enough to give nightmares to any normal human, god, or demon.

Furthermore, there is another element in the East that would surprise many, and that is the secularist or materialist strand. As a philosophical school, the Indian secularists were called Charvaka or Lokayata. They believed that there is no mind or soul, only matter, no former and future life, and personal consciousness is a random event emergent from complexity in the chaotic arrangements of material quanta. One of my favorite sayings of theirs against the theists was, "If you can send offerings to the gods through the fire sacrifice, why give them only a little bit at a time? Why not throw in the entire harvest and then jump in yourself and all go to heaven together?"

"Enlightenment" (buddhahood), as the ultimate evolutionary result of the perfection of mind and body through a continuum of lives, was obviously not a credible goal for them, as they denied any sort of coherent causality. There was no sin or negative evolutionary action for them either, only what you might enjoy and what you could get away with in this life, without any local negative consequence. "Eat, drink, and be merry, for tomorrow we may die and will be nothing!" Beyond their philosophers, Lokayata practitioners were sophisticated urbanites, wealthy and endowed with leisure, and their doings can be discerned in the *Kamasutra* literature, the sophisticated pursuit of pleasure, social and artistic as well as sexual, and in the *Arthashastra* literature, the practical literature of realpolitik, hardball political management theory about how to maximize the wealth and power of the state. These secularists sound very "modern Western," do they not?

China and other Asian states also had all the above variants of cosmologies and attitudes about emotions. But India was the most powerful and seminal of all the Asian cultures in ancient times, due to the subcontinent's relatively greater wealth and size.

But one different element emerged as mainstream in the East, in the Buddhist, Jainist, Yogic and Vedantic Hindu, and Taoist streams of culture. They developed an "Inner Science," an effective depth psychology that understood and condemned enslavement to anger, that connected to a biological theory that discovered an evolutionary multilife perspective. It taught practical paths to conquer the addictive poisons of delusion, anger, and desire, here and now in this precious human life, and thereby enjoy freedom for oneself along with the ability to bring those fruits to others—to demilitarize individuals and societies.

Not that this element is utterly absent in the West. Above the tribal and nationalistic tendencies in the West, in Greece, Egypt, Judea, Rome, and the Northern countries, there is a thin strand within "mystic" Christianity of peaceful universalism, of monastic self-restraint based on the Beatitudes' critique of violence and militarism, a way of seeing the Cross itself as the ultimate critique of Caesar on the one hand and the tribal "Father-God" on the other. It is just that, in the East, amid their own continuing tribal and nationalistic tendencies, there is a relatively much thicker strand in the form of the Buddha-ist, or "Enlightenment-ist" movement. It was a broad movement of peaceful universalism, founded on monastic self-restraint embedded in a much more ancient and prevalent institution that flourished a good seven centuries before Christian monasticism even got started. Due to the relatively greater tolerance of Indian society, this enlightenment movement unfolded close to the mainstream, migrating eventually to all the Asian societies. It was a systematic way of education and self-discipline based on an Inner Science psychology that promised and at least seemed to deliver real freedom from anger, greed, and delusion to the individual, and real nonviolence and relative peacefulness to the society.

In short, to the astonishment of Western, militarism-lens-tinted historians, in the East there is a record of a real, progressive demilitarization of societies that were once just as violent as the Europeans or Americans, and of the attainment of relatively higher levels of peacefulness. Indeed, imperialist historians of previous centuries noted this, but they put it down as "decadence," as what enabled them to conquer the East, as proving their superiority to the inferior, passive, nonviolent, "child-like," "effeminate" Easterners. But in any enlightened definition of culture or civilization, it is precisely the gentle victim, not the violent bully of a conqueror, that is counted as superior.

The arc of this essay travels the route just summarized until it gets back here to this heart of the matter. What may we most realistically consider "anger" to be? How does it work to enslave us and ruin our lives? Is it conquerable? If so, how? Once anger is conquered, can we use the energy it previously monopolized and turn it to activist uses, to shape things and events in more positive ways?

CHAPTER   THREE

What is Anger?

Anger" is an English word, which we must remember when we read about it in the Hebrew and Greek Bible, the Greek Aristotle, or Sanskrit or Tibetan sources—we are reading a translation from some other original word. In the *Oxford English Dictionary* we see that it seems to derive from Old Norse *angr,* which is said to mean "trouble," "affliction," even "pain." This etymology encourages us to say that anger is pain, it comes from feeling pain, and it moves to inflict pain. *Webster's Collegiate Dictionary* has a useful little paragraph on this, after giving the third and active definition,

a strong passion or emotion of displeasure, and usually antago-
nism, excited by a sense of injury or insult. Synonyms: Anger,

ire, rage, fury, indignation, wrath mean emotional excitement induced by intense displeasure. Anger, the comprehensive term of this group, suggests, apart from context, neither a definite degree of intensity nor outward manifestation; ire, dismissed as affected but more intense; rage implies loss of self-control of emotion, often connoting a temporary mental derangement; fury, even more than rage, implies an overmastering passion verging on madness; indignation stresses a deep, intense, often righteous, anger aroused by that which one considers mean, shameful, or the like; wrath may imply either rage or indignation as its emotional basis, but it also implies a desire or intent to avenge or punish, or to get revenge.

I quote this at length because it will help us to understand how authorities can differ about anger, and see how often disagreements are about semantics rather than substance. As the broadest term for this destructive emotional direction, "anger" is clearly the right term for Sanskrit *dvesha*, the key term there, as well as the Greek *orge*, used in Aristotle and the New Testament. It is interesting that both Webster and the *OED* do not mention "hate" as a synonym, glossing "hate" as "intense dislike," cognate with the verbs detest, abhor, abominate, loathe. Thus "hate" seems more a conceptual or mental attitude, while "anger" seems to label an emotional state.

Buddhist psychology uses *dvesha* for both "hate" and "anger," and in fact as the *klesha* ("root vice" or "emotional addiction"), *dvesha* might better be translated "hate-anger," as indeed the Tibetans do with *zhe dvang*, where *zhe* connotes powerful aversion and *dvang* energetic aggression. The fact that hate and anger are so separated in English lets us see at once how there can be two kinds of each, a good one and a bad one. Good hate is thus the dislike of what is truly bad and unpleasant, a perfectly healthy attitude. Bad hate is dislike of what is good and pleasant in another mood or setting. Good anger is aggressive mental movement to destroy a bad or unpleasant obstruction to what is good. Bad anger is an aggressive mental movement to destroy what is good. Without, for the moment, getting into defining good and bad, this is not too complicated.

Aristotle defines anger as an "emotion," in a relatively noncondemning way, as

> an impulse, accompanied by pain, to a conspicuous revenge for a conspicuous slight directed without justification towards what concerns oneself or towards what concerns one's friends—it must always be felt towards some particular individual. It must always be attended by a certain pleasure—that which arises from the expectation of revenge—it has been well said about wrath that "it is far sweeter than slow-dripping honey, clouding the

hearts of men like smoke." It is also attended by a certain pleasure because the thoughts dwell upon the act of vengeance, and the images then called up cause pleasure, like the images called up in dreams. (*Rhetoric,* p. 77, quoting *Iliad,* XVIII, 125–6.)

The Greek philosopher, the teacher of Alexander the Great, is not thinking of anger as any sort of "sin," deadly or otherwise, but sees it as a perfectly normal emotional response and mental attitude. Aristotle gives us a hint about useful anger, in the way he relates it to "fear," which he defines as "a pain or disturbance due to a mental picture of some destructive or painful evil in the future . . . not remote but so near as to be imminent . . . fear is caused by whatever we fear has great power of destroying us or of harming us in ways that tend to cause great pain." He states that anger can banish fear and give persons confidence to deal with what they perceive as a threat, when otherwise they might be paralyzed with fear. Buddhist psychology does not seem to relate fear to anger so neatly, in fact surprisingly not listing fear in its anatomical studies of emotions and attitudes collected in the literature known as *Abhidharma,* or "clear science."

In the Jewish Bible, the angriest person around seems to be God himself. He seems happy enough creating the world and putting Adam and Eve in the garden of Eden along with all the animals. But then when the serpent gets Eve to convince Adam to eat of the forbidden fruit, God gets mad. He curses the serpent to be legless; he curses Eve to suffer pangs of childbirth and to be subordinate to males; he curses Adam with eventual death; and he even curses the ground to not give food without a lot of hard labor. He banishes them all from Eden. After a while he gets mad at Cain for killing his brother out of jealousy. Soon God regrets having made humans, even though they are called "sons of God" and are very godlike, He decides to destroy them all, except for Noah, who is too likable, so he is allowed to escape with family, friends, and animals. Later God gets mad at humans for making a great tower at Babel, so he destroys it and scatters them into groups who speak different languages. God is nice to Abraham for quite a while, until he gets mad about Sodom and Gomorrah and destroys them. Then Isaac, Jacob, and Joseph all do well, though they have to move down to Egypt to survive a famine. They are enslaved in the next generation for some time, until Moses is born and eventually leads them to freedom.

With Moses God goes on a rampage, asking him to ask Pharaoh for freedom, then hardening Pharaoh's heart, then getting some concessions, then again hardening, then blasting the Egyptians, killing their firstborn, then luring them into the sea and destroying their armies. Once across the sea he leads the Jews to the promised land, helping them destroy everyone on the way, more or less. And so on and on.

In sum, God gets angry with humans again and again. He gets angry on behalf of Israel, and sometimes he gets angry at Israel. He's a real punisher. Anyone who was indoctrinated by sacred texts in the image of such a God as the model of ultimate reality personified could be forgiven if he or she thought that anger was an excellent energy and manifestation, as long as one was powerful enough to overcome the enmity such anger stirs up in others.

CHAPTER FOUR

Resigning from Anger
—The Western Way

When we get to Jesus, on one level an archetypally mystical Jewish Rabbi, he models anger as righteous indignation quite strongly in his teaching and challenging of the Roman and Jewish establishments of his day. But he enters into another realm in what may be his core teaching, the "Beatitudes" or the Sermon on the Mount, as recorded in Matthew. (We cannot say such and such is for certain Jesus' core teaching, since the Gospels are all written decades after and codified later by the church establishment, so one can never be sure.) Anyway, the teaching of the Sermon on the Mount is very similar to Buddhist teachings of previous centuries, while the

Savior's life and messianic sacrifice is presented as the fulfillment of the Jewish Bible's predictions of the Jewish Messiah.

What does Matthew's Jesus teach at the core of his teaching? What does his teaching about the root of people's attitudes tell us about anger in Christian tradition? Jesus' main point therein is to reverse all that the worldly think of as power and success. He blesses not the rich but the poor, not the well-companied but the mournful, not the proud but the meek, not the cruel but the merciful, not the conquerors but the peacemakers, not the dominant but the persecuted. The pure in heart, he insists, attain and enjoy the kingdom of heaven. He declares that he fulfills the ancient law of God, and does not break it. But he goes beyond it. Perhaps most important for our context is the following passage.

> You have heard that it was said to those of ancient times, "You shall not murder"; and "whoever murders shall be liable to judgment." [This is of course the ancient law of Moses.] But I say to you that if you are angry with a brother or sister, you will be liable to judgment; and if you insult a brother or sister, you will be liable to the council; and if you say "you fool," you will be liable to the hell of fire. (Matthew, 5:21–22)

Here Jesus gives the difficult teaching of the conquest of anger. He is not content with the ancient "Be angry but do not sin." It is not enough, in the light of what he deems possible for humans, that they merely restrain their outward actions. He wants them to find freedom from anger. He warns them that anger just being present in the mind is enough to bring down condemnation. And a word spoken in anger can become the creator of hell. He goes on in the same way to teach the internalization of the various commandments of body, speech, and mind, demanding that sins and vices be confronted and overcome in the mind, not only in outward action.

He continues in another passage highly pertinent to anger, which should transform first into tolerance, and then into compassion and love;

> You have heard that it was said, "An eye for an eye and a tooth for a tooth." But I say to you, Do not resist an evildoer. But if anyone strikes you on the right cheek, turn the other also; and if anyone wants to sue you and take your coat, give him your cloak as well; and if anyone forces you to go one mile, go also the second mile. Give to anyone who begs from you, and do not refuse anyone who wants to borrow from you. You have heard that it was said, "You shall love your neighbor and hate your enemy." But I say to you, Love your enemies and pray for those who persecute you, so that you may be children of your Father in heaven; for he makes his sun rise on the evil and on

the good, and sends rain on the righteous and the unrighteous. For if you love those who love you, what reward do you have? And if you greet only your brothers and sisters, what more are you doing than others? Do not even the Gentiles do the same? Be perfect, therefore, as your heavenly Father is perfect.

(Matthew, 5:38–48)

These passages are amazing to Buddhists—they sketch out just the progression that, as we will see below, the classic teachers of that tradition have taught for two-and-one-half millennia. First you recognize that anger in the mind alone is a kind of inner murder, a virtual killing of the other who has angered you. For that, just as much or more than for outer, physical murder, you are "liable to judgment." This means that, whether or not you have really committed a murderous act and are socially caught and punished, whether or not there is an all-knowing "God" that will judge and punish, you have committed a negative "evolutionary act" or "karma" in your mind, and the impression left by your act in your own physical and mental continua has reshaped your being in a negative evolutionary direction, which will bring you highly unwanted consequences in the future. Your "killing muscle" has been strengthened, making it more likely you will think "kill" or physically kill again, making you more hated by others wanting vengeance, more prone to provoking others. This will make you more likely to be killed in return—this negative continuum going on in a vicious circle without end, life after life intertwined with other beings involved with you life after life, ending up in a gehenna, a "hell of fire."

Once you realize the absolute loss pertaining to killing or even angrily thinking to do it, you reverse your worldly values. You realize that tolerance, meekness, and gentleness are a supreme evolutionary advantage, breaking the vicious cycle of mutual domination, developing a virtuous cycle of increasing mutual vulnerability and tolerance. Then you are ready to go beyond the law of even justice, eye for an eye, restraining anger to due proportion to the injury, and learn to tolerate injury, even to invite it, creating more and more powerful karmic impressions of mildness and gentleness. You begin to live more and more in the "kingdom of God," the domain of absolute strength, imperturbability, where nothing can harm you because of your ultimate flexibility beyond life and death, bliss beyond pain and pleasure. This is the domain wherein you can love not only your friends but also and equally your enemies, wanting them all to be as happy as you, at the extreme end of the virtuous circle of mutual surrender beyond not only hells of fire but also temporary heavens of superficial pleasure, in the supreme bliss of freedom beyond all dualities such as self and other.

Jesus does not accept the hopeless nature of the struggle against anger and the other deadly sins, addictive vices, or vicious passions. He is not providing support for some later interpreters of Christianity who proclaim their hopeless nature as sinners, thinking that after they have sinned up a storm all life long, they can just believe and call on Jesus, and he will save them from the consequences. No, Jesus tells them they must become perfect, indeed as perfect as God the Father. He demands that they become enlightened, not just faithful. And he underlines this again in another striking passage a little later, which should sober those so-called dedicated followers of Christ who think they can kill, steal, lie, abuse, hoard, and hate in the name of Jesus and then be forgiven just by calling his name:

> Not everyone who says to me, "Lord, Lord," will enter the kingdom of heaven, but only the one who does the will of my Father in heaven. On that day, many will say to me, "Lord, Lord, did we not prophesy in your name, and cast out demons in your name, and do many deeds of power in your name?" Then I will declare to them, "I never knew you; go away from me, you evildoers." (Matthew 7:21–23).

Jesus insists that faith alone, denominational belonging, nominal partisanship, confessional participation, without positive evolutionary action of mind and speech and body, will not suffice for anyone to enter the kingdom, to attain freedom from the fires of anger, the flood of desire, the cage of folly. This precludes those crusaders who kill or incite to kill in Jesus' name, those self-righteous capitalists who squeeze the people for profit to hoard up wealth and then seek redemption by giving to Jesus' church, or those who let their minds wallow in sewers of lust and hatred and idle folly with no attempt at control or liberation, and then seek freedom from consequences by calling for help from omnipotent authority. No, Jesus tells them to "be perfect," just as God is, that to act on the teachings to conquer anger and other vices is to build your house on a rock, and not to act is like building it on sand.

Contemporary with Jesus, the great Stoic philosopher Seneca (ca. 3 B.C.E.–65 C.E.) wrote a brilliant essay on anger, which he calls "this most hideous and frenzied of all the emotions." He says that "some of the wise have described anger as 'brief insanity'—it is just as uncontrolled. Oblivious of decency, heedless of personal bonds, obstinate and intent on anything once started, closed to reasoning or advice, agitated on pretexts without foundation, incapable of discerning fairness or truth, it most resembles those ruins which crash in pieces over what they have crushed." Seneca waxes even more eloquent,

No plague has cost the human race more. You will see slaughter, poisoning, charge and sordid counter-charge in the law-courts, devastation of cities, the ruin of whole nations, persons of princely rank for sale at public auction, buildings set alight and the fire spreading beyond the city walls, huge tracts of territory glowing in flames that the enemy has kindled . . . cities of greatest renown, their very foundations now scarcely discernible—anger has cast them down; deserts, mile after mile without inhabitant—anger emptied them. Look at all those leaders remembered as examples of ill-fortune—anger stabbed one in bed, smote down another amid the solemnities of the banquet, tore a third to pieces in the sight of the law-courts and crowded forum; anger made one the bleeding victim of his parricide son, told another to expose his royal throat to the hand of a slave and ordered a third to stretch spread-eagled in crucifixion. Leave aside the individuals of single executions. Look upon gathered throngs put to the sword, on the military sent in to butcher the populace en masse, on whole peoples condemned to death in an indiscriminate devastation. (Seneca, 1995; pp. 18–19)

Seneca wants to make it clear that there is nothing good about anger—and this as a Stoic, not as a pious Christian with notions of deadly sins, nor as a Buddhist seeking freedom. In defining anger, Seneca quotes Aristotle's definition with approval as "a burning desire to pay back pain." He distinguishes it from mere ferocity, aggressiveness, arousal, and frenzy, which he says also occur in animals. He implies that anger, though an emotion, has therefore some admixture of human "reason," which he denies to animals. This contradicts his earlier statement that anger is insanity and closed to reasoning, but his attempt to separate anger from mere fierce impulse or aggressiveness is reminiscent of the Buddhist definition, wherein anger is an emotional addiction with a conceptual focus, not just raw emotional energy. Seneca rejects the "naturalness" of anger, as the human's nature is social, made for cooperation and tolerance and gentleness, and anger is therefore a harsh distortion of that nature. He rejects the argument that injurers should be angrily punished—so putting anger to good use—since punishment is much more effective if inflicted where appropriate without anger. He cites the supposition, advanced also by Aristotle, that anger is useful, since it is needed to banish fear when facing threat, and gives us the confidence and energy to defend ourselves or attack preemptively, and even that it empowers the intellect to see things clearly. Seneca rejects these ideas with the argument that anger can never serve as the tool of reason and so be applied to useful ends effectively, since its nature is to take over reason, and so ignore all calls for moderation. He likens it to shooting. Once the arrow has been released there is no re-aiming to be done, it must run its course. Examples of people restraining anger in action are dismissed as rather being instances of anger running out of steam and then reason reasserting itself.

He then brings up different kinds of cases in which righteous indignation might be deemed appropriate—when you are at war, when your loved ones are murdered, when your country is attacked, when you see evil-doing people in general. Seneca argues like a Buddhist that in all these cases, prosecution, defense, prevention and punishment are all better served without getting angry, that anger always makes it harder to get things right. What is needed in these situations are courage, justice, endurance, and wisdom; such virtues have no need of borrowing their strength from vicious emotions such as anger. Quoting Aristotle (perhaps unfairly) as likening anger to a useful weapon for just war or noble fighting, Seneca rejects the usefulness of the weapon; it is a breakable sword or a spear with two points, one pointed toward the wielder. He gives the martial artist's observation that the energy of anger is not steady and reliable, it attacks violently at first, but quickly wearies and cannot sustain the fight, giving the example of a snake that emits all its venom on the first bite and then is harmless. Then there are those who consider anger something magnificent, as imparting "greatness of mind." He responds that it gives no greatness but only sometimes the state of "morbid enlargement." And I love his final passage of the first book, which touches on some of our other deadly sins as well:

So there is nothing about anger, not even in the apparent extravagance of its disdain for gods and men, that is great or noble. If anyone does think that anger makes a great mind manifest, he might think the same about self-indulgence—with its wish to be borne on ivory, dressed in purple, roofed with gold, to transfer whole plots of land, enclose whole stretches of sea, turn rivers into cascades and woodlands into hanging gardens. Avarice, too, might betoken a great mind—watching, as it does, over stacks of gold and silver, cultivating estates on a par with provinces. So, too, might lust—it swims across the straits, castrates whole flocks of boys and braves the husband's sword in contempt of death. So, too, ambition—not content with yearly honors. It would, if possible, fill the consul list with one man's name alone, distributing his memorials all over the world. But all these, no matter what lengths they go to or how wide they spread, are narrow, wretched, mean. Virtue alone is exalted and lofty. Nor is anything great which is not at the same time calm.

Seneca too has an interesting analysis of how anger arises:

Our question is whether anger starts with a decision or an impulse, that is, whether it is set in motion of its own accord— or in the same way as most inner events which occur with our full knowledge. Our view is that it undertakes nothing on its own, but only with the mind's approval. To receive an impression of wrong done to one, to lust for retribution, to put together the two propositions that the damage ought not to have been done and that punishment ought to be inflicted, is not the work of a mere involuntary impulse. What we have here is a complex with several constituents—realization, indignation, condemnation, retribution. These cannot occur without the assent by the mind to whatever has struck it.

This will be important to remember, analyzing the anger that is deadly, the mortal sin, the root vice or emotional addiction, as not merely being an emotion, in the sense of an unconscious impulse, but resulting from the combination of emotion arisen from painful experience with a conceptual recognition of the source of the pain and a decision to follow the impulse to attack that source. It is, as Aristotle noted, closely linked with fear, the anticipation of pain, in that fear weakens the will to bear the pain or take measures to avoid it, and so cripples the decision to act, making it seem necessary to the frightened person to explode irrationally to get done what he or she cannot see how to do rationally. Perhaps this is why the militaristic Aristotelians think of anger as necessary for fighting and war, as partially good, since soldiers would be too afraid to join battle if they were acting rationally, so they must explode in anger to throttle their better judgment and attack unreasonably in spite of their reasonable fear. But Seneca claims, as do other classical thinkers, that courage is the source of strength that lifts us out of fear. This presumes that courage is rational energy, fire, heat, power that emerges from the good intention to defend oneself, one's loved ones, one's country, ones principles.

Seneca also works on therapy for anger, though he keeps veering off his theme there to return to the horrors of it. It seems that he both wants to reject the view that anger has some good in it and also feels that the decision that it is bad as being the first and indispensable step in getting rid of it. It is interesting for our purposes that he agrees with Matthew's Jesus (not available to him in any text, though contemporary with him, since Matthew's Gospel is not written until five years after Seneca's death) that humans are perfectible (in the Stoic belief that human reason partakes of the pure reason of Zeus), and so anger can be conquered through discipline and understanding.

A little later, we meet Plutarch (late first century C.E.) and find him aware of and quite in consonance with Seneca, though perhaps less transcendental than the latter or than Jesus. Plutarch defines anger, referring indirectly to Zeno, as

> a kind of conglomerate of emotional seeds. It contains elements extracted from pain and pleasure and arrogance; it has the

gloating pleasure of spite, and also gets its method of grappling from spite, in the sense that the avoidance of its own suffering is not the purpose of its efforts, but it accepts harm to itself while destroying the other person; and one of its ingredients is the form of desire which is the most disagreeable of all, the longing to hurt someone else. (Plutarch, 1992; p. 198)

As we wander through Western literature, these themes persist, not only in the Christian writers, but also in the classical ones. Some favor the Aristotelian school and leave a place for "justified anger," others do not. St. Augustine will have none of it: "It is better to deny entrance to just and reasonable anger than to admit it, no matter how small it is. Once admitted it is driven out again only with difficulty. It comes in as a little twig and in less than no time it grows big and becomes a beam." (S. Schimmel, 1997; p. 91 [quoting St. Francis de Sales, quoting Augustine])

Chaucer gives us a neat analysis of all the "mortal sins," here in translation from Old English (Chaucer, 1981), using the family of words "anger," "hate," "ire," "fury," "wrath," "violence," "vindictiveness," "malice," and "spite." He explains that a "deadly" or "mortal" sin is some act that one loves more than Christ, contrasted with a "venial" sin committed out of not loving Christ enough. He gives an order of importance to the sins, beginning with pride (loving self more than God), envy (loving self more than the neighbor), anger (hating God or neighbor), sloth (depressed laziness, as hatred spills over onto self), avarice (idolizing possessions), gluttony (idolizing food), and lechery (idolizing sex). The way to freedom from these deadly sins begins with sincere repentance, and continues with energetic pursuit of the opposing virtues, respectively: humility; the love of God and neighbor; gentleness, patience, and tolerance; fortitude, strength, magnanimity, faith, and hope; mercy, pity, and charity; abstinence, temperance, shame, and moderation; chastity and continence. Chaucer is quite specific in methodology of repentance, analyzing it into three parts: contrition of heart, confession by mouth, and expiation by deed. He analyzes contrition into six components: (1) conscience or penitence, (2) self-regard, not wishing to be addicted to sins, (3) fear of hellish consequence, (4) regret for goodness lost, (5) remembrance of passion of Christ, (6) hope for forgiveness, the gift of grace, and the glory of heaven. Confession must have four conditions: (1) done in remorseful bitterness of heart, (2) done speedily, (3) done fully, (4) done without lying to cover up. Expiation is performed through almsgiving and bodily asceticism.

As to anger, Chaucer holds there to be a good anger, the zeal to do good when enraged by wickedness, gently, without bitterness, not against man but against the deed of man. The bad anger is of two types: sudden anger, the heating of the blood, which is only venial, being a quick loss of control of reason, and the mortal, fully wicked anger, which has malice aforethought from sullenness of heart, which, in turn, is the devil's furnace, combined with pride and a wish for vengeance. Anger's antidote is patience, which is of four kinds; patience at being verbally abused, having one's property ruined, suffering bodily injury, and being enslaved or overworked.

CHAPTER FIVE

Resigning from Anger —The Buddhist Way

There are many more analyses of anger in the vast library of Western psychology accumulated by the Christian monastics and later, academic moralists. It is amazing how thorough they are, how reminiscent of the Buddhist Abhidharmic psychology. The Buddhist analysis of the causes of suffering is not oriented toward faith in an omnipotent God, since Buddha reported on his encounter with the "Creator" God (Brahma, as he was called in India at that time) that he was neither omnipotent, nor omniscient, nor did he create the universe after all.

The Buddha proclaimed the root cause of suffering to be the mental addiction to delusion, ignorance, or misknowledge. This delusion was the misperception of the self as an absolute, independent, thing-in-itself, which corresponds with misperceiving everything else as having absolute, independent essence or substance. This deep-seated delusion has instinctual and conceptual forms, and it causes suffering by putting the person in the hopeless situation of being a fixed, absolute, intrinsically real self versus a real universe, inevitably losing out to that universe of beings and things through sickness, aging, death, pain, loss, torment, and so on. This root delusion of self-addiction is actually rather close to the deadly sin of pride ("love of self more than God"), if "God" is interpreted as the vast energy of life.

I should explain here how the "enlightenment" called buddhahood is understood as the overcoming of delusion. The Buddha discovered in himself the delusional, self-absolutizing habit-pattern at instinctual and intellectual levels, and took up the challenge to verify if he really did exist in that substantial, unique, independent manner. He dissected his mindbody complex with intensive critical insight and one-pointed concentration, and eventually broke through the delusion by failing to discover any absolute self within. He then avoided reifying that failure by taking mere nothingness as a self, as some modern materialist thinkers have done. Instead he understood the ramifications of that failure as being the absolute relativity of the self, its total interconnectedness, its illusoriness or virtuality, and so on. This freed him to develop his relative, virtual self as a living work in progress, actually limitless in horizons of excellence, given endless time for evolution.

I could say more, since this is the essence of the Buddha's great scientific breakthrough and personal evolutionary achievement, but this hopefully gives the basic idea. It is crucial for understanding the conquest and subsequent transformation of the anger energy.

The second mental addiction that follows the root misknowledge or self-delusion is the desire addiction, which includes lust, avarice, and gluttony. Once one feels oneself to be a lone, unique, separate self in confrontation with the universe, one wants to incorporate as much of the universe as possible into oneself, to even the odds, so to speak, as futile as the attempt may be—imagine trying to swallow the entire universe!

The third mental addiction going along with this deluded, discontented state is the anger addiction—anger at the universe for resisting being incorporated into oneself, anger born of fear of oneself becoming swallowed up by the universe, anger that wants to destroy the opposing universe once and for all in the defense of one's delusional self.

These three—delusion, desire, and anger—are the three poisons that are on all forms of psychological lists. Next comes pride, which is the self-preoccupation that follows upon delusion's self-absolutization, and then good old familiar envy, the resentment of the happiness or fortune of others.

In an alternative listing of six root addictions in the early Inner Science (Abhidharma) systems, after delusion, desire, anger, and pride, the last two addictions are fanatic views and doubts. These cognitive addictions describe our deluded mind's habits, the one being to become fixated upon a rigid, absolutist, dogmatic faith, conviction, or ideology, and the other being to wallow in confused perplexity, not able to focus the mind in any direction at all, without feeling free from directions. The former blocks critical inquiry and the latter prevents liberating insight.

Focusing in particular upon the root anger, we see that the analysis locates it as arising from the base of the self-other-absolute-separation delusion, which is what makes it an emotional addiction rather than a raw emotion. This is reminiscent of Seneca's judgment that anger is only present in humans, since animal rage is devoid of any conceptual component, and true anger is always emotion combined with conceptual calculation aiming at a specific destruction.

After the six root addictions, there are twenty derivative addictions (though other inner science systems posit fifty, even one hundred and eight, so all these systems should be understood as heuristic and not dogmatic inventories). In the best known of these systems, branching off the root of anger, there are four derivative addictions: aggression, vindictiveness, malice, and violence. All four are driven by anger, the first being when anger moves mind, speech, or body in the direction of assault on others; the second being the thirst for revenge against the hated enemy; the third being the wish to speak woundingly; and the fourth being the general inclination to cause harm to others.

Finally, there is another analysis that works with the fivefold scheme, usually kept esoteric, at least until recent times, wherein the root addictions are conquered and their energies transformed into the basic energies of a liberated life. The root of these root addictions is delusion. When delusion is destroyed by understanding and wisdom, then the other addictive energies, desire, anger, and so on, can also be transmuted into wisdoms—pure energies that are creative and blissful rather than harmful and painful. Hence they are satisfying and enjoyable, no longer addictive. Remember, "addictive" means something that promises satisfaction and does not deliver it for long, causing you to want it more and more and making you more and more frustrated.

Once wisdom has released you from the self-absolutizing delusion, the energy of solidification of subject and object becomes relativized and can be wielded creatively, and delusion itself becomes the "mirroring wisdom," diamond white, the element earth, and the process of materiality. The desire addiction then becomes the energy of connectedness, the individuating wisdom, ruby red, the element fire, and the process of discernment. The pride addiction becomes the equalizing wisdom, topaz gold, the element water, and the process of sensation. The envy addiction becomes the all-accomplishing wisdom, emerald green, the element wind, and the process of mental functions. Finally, the anger addiction becomes the ultimate reality perfection wisdom, sapphire blue, the element space, and the consciousness process.

These deep mental and emotional energies thus are re-envisioned by the enlightened, delusion-free being as wisdom energies, ways of awareness expressing its inconceivable blissful union with all of life and death as color and form and matter and mind, impelled by liberated compassion to reshape the universe to enfold all sensitive beings in positive environments of optimal access to their own supreme potential.

However marvelous these blissful visions of the deep world-reweaving of Tantric psychology, none of this can take place until delusion is transformed into wisdom. So first, addictions such as anger must be tamed or conquered, so their energies can be safely redeployed.

CHAPTER SIX

The Yoga of Anger Transcendence

How can we resign from anger? How does the great saint and sage Shantideva teach us to do it? The first step is to determine that we must. Basically, "anger" refers to a state of being and a way of doing that we are much better off eliminating.

> Whatever my virtuous deeds may be,
> Venerating buddhas, generosity and so on,
> Amassed over a thousand aeons—
> All are destroyed in a moment of anger.

Anger is viewed here as an emotional addiction rather than as a sin. "Sin" goes along with "crime" as a transgression of a law, with punishment as its consequence, by the monotheistic "God" in case of sin, by society in case of a crime. An addiction is a habit that has become compulsive, is not in the control of the addict, and has its own negative consequence in a causal physical and mental process. When its result continues beyond the single life of a single individual, it can be fairly termed "evolutionary," whether that evolutionary continuum is seen as a physical process of habit encoded in physical genes that produce new but affected bodies (of some other beings), or as a psychophysical process in which the habit encodes a "psychic" gene that shapes the production of new bodymind complexes of an ongoing individual continuum.

The absolute first step in the yoga of patience is coming to the decision that anger is bad, evil, negative, an addiction, or even a sin. As in quitting any addiction, the mind must become determined in its resolve to eliminate this negative attitude and emotion. To reach this point, anger must have a precise definition, a boundary we draw between anger and related impulses, emotions, or energies. Anger happens when irritation, annoyance, disapproval, and so forth suddenly burst into an irresistible impulse to respond in a harmful manner to the perceived source of those feelings. You are no longer the master of the mental, verbal, or bodily acts then committed; you are not "expressing your anger"; you have become the involuntary instrument of your anger. For example, who could be angry with a bodhisattva, a completely altruistic person, if they were in control of their feelings? You can only feel sheer anger, hate, the urge to violence, when you lose your good sense, are inflamed with rage. This "madness," insane in its fury, destroys all the evolutionary progress you might have made in a long, long effort. Shantideva uses the extreme example of being angry with a bodhisattva. In the Western sense, it might be compared with anger against Jesus, Mary, Moses, Muhammad, or God himself. It means being angry with the source of all goodness, biting the hand that feeds you. It is patently self-destructive.

> There is no evil as harmful as anger,
> No discipline as effective as patience,
> Thus by all possible means I should
> Cultivate patience with intensity.

Deciding that anger always harms, its opposite needs to be understood as unfailingly helpful. The opposite of anger ultimately is love and compassion, the will to help others not to suffer and to be happy. However, it is pushing ourselves too far to insist on immediately switching from anger and hate to compassion and love. There is a middle ground, the ground of tolerance, patience, forbearance, and forgiveness. We grow angry when we are harmed, or think we are. We might still be irritated but will not lose ourselves to anger as long as we can tolerate the irritation, be patient with the harm, forbear from reacting, and even forgive the injury. So the positive resolve is to cultivate tolerance and patience.

> Keeping the mind wounded by anger,
> I will never experience peace.
> I will have no joy or happiness,
> Will lose my sleep, writhing with frustration.

When one has been injured by something or someone, the anger one feels is a second injury from within; it is another wound in itself. Your mind cannot rest as anger stirs within you to revenge yourself on the injurer. Things that ordinarily cause you pleasure, even joy, the face of your beloved, good food, enchanting entertainment, sensual delight, all of them immediately lose their appeal the minute you become angry. When really angry, you cannot even fall asleep, your mind goes over the injury again and again, and plots how to retaliate in kind or worse.

Anger spoils relationships in which there should be great reciprocity. Even when others depend on you and receive from you their livelihood and dignity, they will hate you and wait for a chance to hurt you and even destroy you if you constantly subject them to your anger.

> Anger wears out friends and relatives;
> "Though pleased by my gifts, they never trust me!"
> In sum, there is no way to live happily
> While burning with the fire of anger.

Anger is like fire—it burns you, and it burns others. You cannot be happy when others are closed off to you, which they will be if they perceive you as harmful and wounding, as you always are when you are angry. Adding up these thoughts you can decide that anger is always hurtful, spoiling even things that are normally good.

> Anger—my real enemy—
> Creates such sufferings as these.
> But whoever controls and conquers it,
> Finds happiness here and hereafter.

This is the big decision, that anger itself is your greatest enemy. It causes you the most harm, wounds you from within, kills your happiness, and is especially hard to defend against since it comes from within yourself—it actually masquerades *as* yourself. Once you understand this, it simplifies your struggle to discover happiness. This decision gives you a key to happiness. For, since your main enemy is within, is one single source, you can turn on it, find its root, learn its manifestations and armor yourself against them, and work to uproot it. Then you will be free of its harm. You can conquer it, bit by bit, and realistically achieve the happiness you seek.

This is the radical discovery of Buddhist psychology. You don't have to resign yourself to ordinary suffering, to being always unconscious of what is really going on, helpless before not only society and space and time and others, but more importantly before your own inner drives, impulses, and demands. You need not give up and allow yourself to be buffeted here and there by passions and angers. You can become conscious of what you were formerly unconscious. You can understand your drives, see where they come from, block the source, and divert the energy for your own use. You can resist all imperatives and learn to wield the underlying energies. You can reclaim those energies for your life, for your happiness and the happiness of your loved ones.

Next we must understand the mental mechanics of anger.

Anger finds its food in the mental discomfort
I feel, faced with the unwanted happening

And the blocking of what I want to happen;

It then explodes and overwhelms me.

The definition of "anger," both as a Western mortal, deadly, or capital vice or sin and as an Eastern root mental addiction, essentially includes its ability to carry you away. It occurs when the addictive passion demolishes our reason and common sense, and our mind, speech, and body become its tools. The insight Shantideva shares with us here is that before real anger happens, there is a "mental discomfort" or frustration that comes from seeing things happen you don't want, or seeing what you do want being thwarted. Though you become more and more irritated with these situations, you are still reasonable. The key trick is to intervene, mentally, verbally, or physically to dissipate the discomfort, to engage the situation energetically, before you explode and lose control to your anger and become its tool.

Seeing that, I should carefully eliminate

That food that gives life to the enemy;

For that enemy has no activity at all

Other than causing me harm.

Thus, to prevent the fuel of anger from reaching the point of combustion, you can either intervene in the outer situation or deal internally with your reaction. If you act outwardly, you can be energetic, even aggressive (since anger is not merely aggression but rather an extreme kind of aggression), to make what you want happen or to prevent what you don't want from happening. Your active engagement will be much more effective when you are reasonable and in control of your energy than it will be when you are out of control and prone to overreact. However, it is always possible that you can't affect the outcome anyway, and what you most fear takes place, or what you most hope does not. In that case, you must turn and intervene in your inner world, in your mind.

> Whatever happens, I must not allow
> My cheerfulness to be disturbed.
> Being unhappy won't fulfill my wish,
> And will lose me all my virtues.

Here the intervention is to prevent the discomfort or frustration from becoming intolerable. You must remain happy, cheerful, content. How do you do that? There are many ways. You distract yourself by counting your blessings, thinking about how it could be even worse. You look more deeply at the picture that is bothering you, see how you can use the disadvantage of your thwarted hopes to your advantage, and develop your tolerance and strength. You see through your sense of certainty about what's wrong and see it from other perspectives. Minimally, you realize that letting yourself get all freaked out is not going to improve the situation but simply add to your unhappiness—add an inner pain to an outer pain. This is crucial, since you are dealing with an addiction. The addict is seduced by the addictive substance by feeling that it will help relieve their bad feeling. Likewise, anger approaches your mind by presenting itself as a helpful energy, "This is just unacceptable, outrageous! Let us explode with fury and our fiery energy will burn away the obstacle, will clear up the situation. Maybe things didn't always work out in the past, but what else can you do about this pain!" This addiction to a mental habit is more subtle than the addiction to a physical substance that promises a state of mind. The mental habit comes to you as your own new state, as the imperative of your own nature, hence all the more irresistible. The addict has had experience of the rush, the high, and the dreadful comedown after everything has gotten worse, but in the moment of temptation, this tends to be ignored for the promise of the rush. This is where the recognition of anger as an enemy, the original decision from whence the yoga of taming anger begins, becomes all-important.

Why be unhappy about something
If you can do something about it?

If nothing can be done,

What does being unhappy help?

This is a classic maxim. When you are frustrated, you can intervene aggressively in a situation before you get angry, doing so cheerfully and with a joyous energy. When there is nothing to be done, then you can intervene within yourself, reminding yourself not to add to your unhappiness by adding madness to your frustration.

Winged Yidam, eighteenth century.

Winged Heruka, eighteenth century.

Vajrabhairava, eighteenth century.

Dance apron depicting face of Mahakala, seventeenth century.

Guru Drakpo, or "the Wrathful Teacher," nineteenth century.

Bonpo Dharmapala, eighteenth century.

Protective talisman chart with yellow tortoise as emanation of Manjushri,
nineteenth century.

Manjushri, eighteenth century.

CHAPTER SEVEN

Tolerant Patience

Unwanted for me and my friends
Are suffering, contempt,
Harsh words and disrepute;
For enemies it is just the opposite.

Just remember what anger is, how it relates to injury and suffering. It's amazing how things that make me angry, that cause me suffering, pain, discomfort, and embarrassment, still please me when they happen to someone I consider an enemy. I want them to have the very suffering I don't want.

Cause for happiness sometimes happens;
Causes of suffering are very many.

But without suffering there is no transcendence,

So, my mind, you must be brave!

It is so much easier to suffer than to be happy, since the causes of suffering seem more plentiful than the causes of happiness. Hence you are going to suffer more. Logically, the only way you can begin to find a more abundant happiness is to discover a way to use the usual causes of suffering and turn them into causes of happiness. Then you can use your experiences of suffering to develop the transcendent mind, the mind oriented toward freedom, the mind that renounces superficial pleasures in the quest of reliable happiness. Then the plentiful causes of suffering will give you plentiful causes for happiness, reliable happiness based on freedom. So you seek suffering to strengthen your enduring patience, your power of tolerance, which leads to freedom, which makes happiness possible. "That which does not kill me makes me stronger!" said Nietzsche. "No pain, no gain," say body builders.

Pointlessly, penitents and flagellants

Endure the sensations of cuts and burns;

Why then, my mind, are you afraid

To suffer for the sake of freedom?

"What? Are we entering the zone of masochism here? Are we

seeking suffering and pain as cures for anger? Not likely to work, too weird!" No, of course you are not being masochists, people who seek pleasure through experiencing pain due to a deep sense of self-loathing. You are not seeking fleeting pleasure through suffering. You are seeking suffering in order to develop transcendent detachment, renunciation of fleeting pleasure, in order to achieve freedom. So you encourage yourself by noting that religious fanatics, masochists, and vain body-worshipers develop a great resistance to pain to achieve their entirely illusory goals. If they can do it for an unsatisfactory goal, you can do it for the greatest goal of all. After all, transcendent tolerance means freedom from fear of any suffering, the only enduring happiness, logically speaking.

> There is nothing which does not become
> Easier to bear through constant practice;
> Thus, by practicing with little pains,
> You should learn to endure great pains.

Gradual development of tolerance does work, it can be seen in all disciplines of body and mind for whatever end, mundane or transcendent.

> Who has not experienced this with accidental pains,
> Bites of insects and of snakes,

Pangs of thirst and hunger and so on,
And irritations such as rashes?

It is just common sense in daily life. Better than scratching an itch is healing the itch to make it go away.

I should not become impatient
With such as heat, cold, rain, and wind,
Sickness, death, bondage, and blows;
For it only adds to the hurt.

Normally we become irritated and frustrated with discomforts from the elements and the natural processes of our vulnerable impermanent life. These frustrations can build into explosions of anger, hating the rain, screaming at the wind, writhing with fury that we have caught this or that disease, suffered this or that assault or accident, shaking our fist at God, fate, Buddha, or our parents when death confronts us. But what is the point? The anger-reaction does not affect the elements or nature or any divine power. It merely adds internal suffering and stress to outer suffering and pressure.

Some become more brave and heroic
When they see their own blood spurt;

Others feel faint and even pass out,
Just when they see another bleed.

These things come from the character of one's mind,
Whether its habit is brave or timid;
Therefore I should disregard injuries
And not let sufferings get to me.

Looking at other people, you can see how some are brave and heroic under duress and in pain, while others succumb to the same circumstances. Obviously you admire the brave and despise the fearful, so you should resolve to cultivate your bravery.

Even though they experience sufferings,
The wise don't let the mind cloud or disturb;
In making war on the addictions,
The battle will bring much harm.

After all, you are in a battle with the vices and addictions, here especially the addiction to anger, and you cannot expect to win such a major conflict without taking some serious blows. Anger uses you to dish out hard knocks to all around you. When you turn on it, you must expect it to turn on you. So you must harden yourself against it. When it turns on you it wants to make you suffer. If you have learned to tolerate suffering as natural without taking offense or taking it personally, then you are fortified against whatever anger can do to you. It cannot win you over, cannot make you angry, and so in this place of great endurance, great inner tolerance, you are finding the way to freedom.

> Truly victorious heroes
> Disregard all sufferings
> And conquer enemies such as anger—
> The rest just slaughter corpses.

Heroism in battle is a simile for the hero in the battle against the enemy anger. Anger and other mental addictions are the truly worthy enemies, whose defeat brings the truly worthy fruit of freedom. They can only be overcome by you when you disregard whatever pain you may suffer in battle with them. You have true heroism then, a heroism beyond death and ordinary self-centered life. Mundane heroes who fight and kill other beings are themselves fueled by anger, are the minions of anger, and they slay zombie-like bodies of enemies who themselves are but the tools of anger. Their anger that drives them onto the field against you has already taken away their lives of freedom, your anger makes you a zombie in its cause. You are a corpse of a hero killing corpses, both of you defeated by the real enemy, anger.

> Further, suffering has its benefits;
> Being tired of it dispels our arrogance,
> It stirs our compassion for cyclic creatures,
> It makes us shun vice and love virtue.

You are now confirmed in the first level of patience, the tolerance of suffering developed through the discipline of conscious suffering, learning to use suffering as a spur to transcendent freedom. In your campaign for patience, primarily to conquer anger, you have also found how to use suffering to counter pride and arrogance, and also how to identify with other addicted and suffering beings, empathizing with their suffering and developing compassion for them, the will to free them also.

CHAPTER EIGHT

Insightful Patience

I am not angry with the major sources
Of sufferings, ill-humors such as bile,
So why am I angry with mental beings,
All driven by conditions as they are?

Having incorporated the level of patience developed through cultivating endurance, you must mobilize your analytical mindfulness to take it farther, into the territory of active forbearance based on insight. Anger always burns within a framework, a conceptual targeting that springs from the habitual, even instinctual, exaggerated reification of the self and objectification of the other. In relation to persons with whom you get angry, you especially focus on their intentions. Though this normally operates unconsciously and automatically, you absolutize a personality in your enemy, projecting from your own absolutized sense of self, and you attribute a malevolent intention to the self of that enemy, thinking he ruthlessly wishes to harm you. You then feel paranoia about that, you fear what that enemy may do, and your anger explodes preemptively, offering you the desperate promise to remove the threat. Here, Shantideva takes note of how, while seeming to be a naturally explosive force of nature, anger actually operates within a habitual discriminative framework. When a bile condition makes you feverish and sick, when the elements cause harm, earthquakes, floods, fires, and windstorms, you do not get angry at bile, earth, water, fire, or air. Your choice of a being with a mind as an enemy, assumed to be just like you, is therefore based on your projecting an independent agency into that being that has chosen, is choosing, or will choose to harm you. When you bring a more focused mindfulness to bear on the situation, when you analyze the realities of yourself, your enemy, the situation, you can quickly see how the enemy is simply an automaton like the earth or a river, his behavior is driven by unconscious impulses and attitudes, just like your own. He has no independence of will at all, but is a helpless victim of his inner drives, just like you.

> As all the while unwillingly,
> Their illnesses inevitably occur,
> So all the while unwillingly,
> Their mental addictions arise compulsively.

Just as bile naturally and mechanically produces heat diseases in the body (as well as anger diseases in the mind) without having any independent willful agency, so an unenlightened mental being is driven to anger by his mental addictions, delusion, lust, anger, and so forth, themselves operating mechanically without willful intent. The choice of "bile" here is significant—in Buddhist medicine "bile" is the humoral analogue of the physical element of fire and the mental poison of anger.

> Not thinking "I should be furious!"
> People helplessly feel fury;
> And not thinking "I must create (fury)!"
> Fury itself automatically arises.

People under the spell of the anger-addiction do not will themselves to manifest anger, they simply explode with anger—though you might think "I should get angry with this or that!" before you get angry, the very nature of anger is that it takes hold of you and deprives you of free will and intelligent choice. Similarly when anger has arisen in rage and fury, it does so without itself having any free agency that chooses to rage. Just as fire does not choose to burn the next log but does so automatically, yourself and your anger, your enemy and his anger are mechanical processes without conscious intent.

Whatever evils can be found
And the various kinds of vice,
All arise by the force of conditions,
And not willfully at all.

Swiftly your analytic mindfulness penetrates to insight, as you see through the reified perception of free agency in evil actions or mental addictions and see things as the inconceivable network of impersonal causes and conditions.

Those conditions gathered together
Have no intention "let us produce harm!"
Nor does their product, harm itself, intend
"I am going to be produced!"

The network of interconnected things and processes lack any personalizable agency that intends you harm and so you have no real target for your anger that you can consciously pick out as the ultimate source of your suffering and so realistically gain happiness by destroying.

Even the postulated agents—soul-stuff,
And the theoretically imagined (self),
Would never act thinking voluntarily,
"I must arise as the cause of harm!"

Theories of soul and essential self in persons and things that religions and philosophies imagine are always posited as absolutes, by definition irreducible, unchanging, nonrelational, and therefore cannot rationally be considered as relationally thinking or acting agents.

> Since such ("soul" or "self") are unproduced and nonexistent,
> So also is their will to produce (harm or any action),
> Since their focus on their object must be permanent,
> It could never eventuate (in action).

In the context of pure wisdom, this consideration leads into the sophisticated metaphysical critical reasoning so highly developed in the Buddhist universities of India and Tibet, where every conceivable (and inconceivable) elaboration of absolute self has been investigated and critiqued. Here the target is anger, so there is no need to engage in such analysis at length. Suffice it to say that such a permanent, indeed absolute, partless, nonrelational entity as immortal soul or self could not be produced by any conditional process but must be unconditional and even unproduced, like space. Hence, it can also not participate in relational, conditional processes, such as thinking or acting.

> If the self were permanent (as claimed),
> It clearly must be inactive just like space,

> Even on encounter with other conditions
> What could it do without changing itself?

Further thought-experiment also sees the picture of a permanent, absolute self not fitting with any picture of relational things, as encountering something as changing itself, as interacting with other relational things, hence showing its implausibility as an existent.

> And if when acted upon it stays the same as before,
> Then what would the action have affected?
> Though we say "this is the action of this!"
> What could possibly be its relation (to anything)?

Here a nonrelational absolute self imagined as present in the midst of relational things drops out of possibility, and the network of relational things emerges as inconceivably free of any nonrelational essences, substances, selves, or any sort of independent thing. This freedom is experienced by such insight, and such insight erodes the sense of absolute self at the core of your self-experience, which is what anger can grip on to and present its own impulses as absolute imperatives.

> Thus everything is in the power of other things
> Themselves in the power of still others;

Knowing that, I will never be angry
With things which are unreal as phantoms.

Insight empowers patience by critically releasing your perceptions from absolutizing the whole discriminative structure within which anger can control you—your "self," the "enemy," the "harm," and the "revenge"—all these entities emerge as constructions by your mental habits. This enables you to unlock the cage of seeming inevitability about what has really happened and what you must really do. Everything begins to hold a tinge of unreality, fluidity, and you achieve a different level of flexibility of response. Where before it seemed you must be angry at what really is too much to bear, now you are enabled to be patient and more careful about perceiving and responding, since you can see things external and internal from many other angles.

"If all were unreal, then what is eliminated by whom?
Surely eliminating anger would be irrational?"
It is not impractical to eliminate anger, if you want
To interrupt the continuous stream of suffering.

But then, you object, "Why should we bother with disciplining anger? Even anger is unreal, the enemy is unreal, I am unreal, so whatever I do doesn't matter any more!" Sure it's all unreal, yet unreal you still unreally experience unreal suffering! "Unreal" just means that what had seemed absolute, intrinsically real, is unreal as absolute and hence only relatively real, which frees you to take responsibility for reshaping things into a better pattern of interaction. "Unreal" refers to the quality of how things exist and does not mean that they are utterly nonexistent. Relative things certainly do not exist as absolutes, but that means they do exist relatively. Since in our relative existence, we suffer horribly, and anger causes much destruction that aggravates suffering, it is entirely practical to get rid of anger.

> Thus if I see enemy or friend
> Do something wrong,
> I will keep my good cheer, thinking,
> "This comes from mechanical conditions."

By developing the patience born of insight, the tolerance aware of the unrealities and realities of things, you can prevent the frustration about things not going right or things going wrong from bursting into anger, staying cheerful by reflecting on the conditionality of all things, that they happen mechanically and so can be engaged calmly and coolly to change their course from negative to positive.

> If it was voluntarily happening,
> Since no one wants to suffer,

No embodied being whatsoever
Would ever experience suffering.

Driving home the point, confirming the helplessness of beings, even your enemies, you realize how suffering only comes about because of the helpless confusion and mental addictions that beings are caught in, which deprive them of any freedom of choice or will.

Through carelessness,
People hurt themselves with thorns and so on,
And to win a mate and so on,
They become obsessed and wasted.

Survey the senseless acts of people and you will soon realize they do not know what they do, as Jesus so famously said.

Some kill themselves jumping off cliffs,
Taking poison and harmful food.
Many recklessly destroy themselves
Engaging in unvirtuous acts.

Look at the people who destroy themselves with anger turned against themselves. How is that going to help them in any way?

Why would they do that if they were in any real sense in control of themselves?

> If in the power of emotional addictions
> They kill even their cherished selves,
> How would they fail to cause harm
> To the bodies of other beings?

If they harm and kill themselves driven helplessly by mental addictions, naturally they cannot be expected not to harm and kill others when directed toward them by anger.

> Thus compelled by addictions,
> When they try such things as killing me,
> Perhaps it's hard to feel compassion,
> But what's the point of getting angry?

It might be hard right away to feel compassion for someone who is trying to kill you or harm you. You may be gripped by fight or flight reactions, you may practically need to defend yourself and have no time to feel sorry for your delusional attacker, but why bother to explode in anger? Save your energy for the most effective rational response to avoid the harm, to cool down the enemy with the most efficient means.

If it is natural for the foolish
To cause harm to others,
It is wrong to get angry with them,
Like resenting fire for burning.

When things catch fire, you give maximum attention to putting it out, using all reasonable methods at your disposal to do so as quickly as possible. You do not first feel bitterly angry at the fire, shout and scream at it, curse its name and so on. You think of that as a waste of time and energy. So you need not bother to get angry with the unenlightened when they harm you, just make every effort to minimize or avoid the harm.

Even if beings are gentle-natured
And the evil of harm is occasional,
It is still wrong to be angry;
Like resenting space for filling with smoke.

If you have the insight that sensitive beings are gentle in nature, since they above all seek to avoid suffering themselves and hence prefer not to provoke others into dangerous reactions by causing them suffering, you might feel that they are violating their own nature when they are angry and harmful and might feel anger is appropriate since the harm that they inflict is unnatural. But when your lungs burn with smoke when the fire doesn't draw, do you get angry with the usually airful space in the room that becomes filled with smoke? No, you cough and hold your breath and try to open the flue, douse the fire, or flee the room. Anger accomplishes nothing.

> Though sticks and so on really hurt me,
> I get angry with the thrower;
> But he is also an instrument moved by anger,
> So I am only rightly angry with anger.

Finally, now that through mindful insight you can see events from various angles without fixating on one absolute perspective that justifies the absolute reaction of anger, you can discern that when someone hits you with a stick, you are not angry at the stick, you are not angry with the hand, you are not angry with the forearm muscle, the bicep, the shoulder, the neck, the face of the hitter—you are angry with the person who intentionally hurts you and hits you with the stick. Your anger focuses on the agency in the person as a conceptual choice. You absolutize that agency as ill-intentioned, and you demonize that enemy, and only then does your anger explode to destroy that enemy. But now that you know the other person is helplessly the tool of his own anger, just as the stick is helplessly the tool of his hand and brain, then you can only be angry with the mental addiction that drives him. You can be angry with his anger, with anger itself. But anger at anger must aim to destroy anger. And anger can only destroy anger by not allowing it entry into the mind. Anger is only destroyed by not getting angry! Effective anger at anger can only become the energy of tolerance.

CHAPTER NINE

Forgiving Patience

Long ago I inflicted
Harm of this kind on beings,
So causing injury to them—
Now this harm comes back to me.

In order to get to the very roots of anger, we must go deeper into
the inconceivability of relational reality, into the web of evolutionary interconnection of sensitive beings through infinite time and
space. We need this larger perspective, because only in the infinite
context can we see all things as causally and conditionally interconnected without any limited, supposedly absolute frame of refer-
ence. We must get beyond "first beginning," "uncaused cause,"
"final limit," and so on, and free ourselves from the projections of

egocentric humans who need to feel contained, who want to hide from the vastness of infinity. To catch the root of anger, in order to uproot its hold over us, where in vast infinity do we seek the original source of suffering, harm, injury, and hence the target of self-protective action? Obviously the answer is within ourselves. We ourselves are what we have at hand. We ourselves are responsible to ourselves. We have primary access to ourselves. We can do something about ourselves. While we may discover that we ourselves in our true nature are just as infinite as the rest of the world, perhaps are not strictly different from the rest of the infinite universe ultimately, nevertheless, it is most useful to approach that infinity through ourselves. Our anger comes from within. Our patience comes from within. Our delusion controls us from within. Our wisdom liberates us from within. So we must take responsibility for creating our own worlds. Our delusion that absolutely separates self and other creates our world of suffering. Our anger invests that divided world of self and other with destructiveness, and turns it into a world of fear and danger. So when anything bad happens to us, the effective move is to go after the source within ourselves. Sitting and blaming the world of others will do no good, it only strengthens our sense of helplessness, since we cannot control others, only ourselves.

So we become creative at last and we joyfully blame ourselves, we purposefully blame the victim to overcome being the victim. Blaming the victim does not deepen our victimization—it frees us from victimization. We take responsibility for everything, and so take command of everything. "OK, I was harmed. I harmed others in the past, so I was harmed now. How excellent I am getting rid of that consequence! Now I will never harm them again, so I will not be harmed. I will avoid the consequences of other past harms I committed by helping others so energetically, it will outweigh the weight of previous harm."

> His weapon and my body
> Both are causes of my suffering.
> He made the weapon, I the body—
> With whom should I be angry?

When the stick descends on my body, two things collide, stick and body. He picked up the stick and made it into a weapon, but I created a body sensitive to such pain and put it in his way. He sees it as a threat to him, as an obstruction to his happiness, so he wants to beat it down out of his way. I created one of the two things that collided. It was created by my delusion, which creates its apparent solidity and separateness from the other world, my anger, which creates its ugliness, its apparent dangerousness to my enemy, and my desire, which creates its appetites that threaten to consume things he wants. So I should redirect my anger to these deeper sources of my suffering, caused by my getting in the way of this person with his stick.

> Blind with craving, if I cling
> To this human form so prone to suffering,
> Agonizing to the touch like an open sore,
> Whom should I hate when it is hurt?

Again, my body is so sensitive, so weak, so needy, so different from this other, is such a body not the thing I should be upset with and should do something about? What can I do about my body? I can transform it into an enlightened body. An enlightened body is the body of a person of transcendent wisdom, who knows experientially that there is ultimately no difference between self and other, yet is relatively responsible for being relatively different according to the perceptions of unenlightened others. An enlightened body is free of desire for union with others, since it is the manifestation of someone who knows self and other are already united. An enlightened body is not perceived as a threat by others, since it appears beautiful to them, free of any harmful impulse or appearance of harmful capacity. An enlightened body is more light about its living, more flexible in its responses, so inwardly blissful that its sensory sensitivity is also more variable, less determined, free not to be agonized even when aware of pain, completely unafraid even of death, which it perceives as merely a transformation of a peripheral level of manifestation. It is hard to imagine such a body, of course, but it is useful to imagine such a body, to entertain the evolutionary goal of transforming the unenlightened body into a body of bliss, seeing its inadequacies as responsible for its suffering, seeing it therefore as susceptible to limitless improvement.

> The foolish don't want suffering,
> Yet thirst after suffering's causes,
> And so hurt themselves by their own vices;
> What's to resent in others?

The foolish are the unenlightened, the self-centered, who try to run away from suffering and toward happiness, fleeting as it may always turn out to be. Addicted to their desire for pleasure, they thirst for it, in denial about the fact they constantly experience dissatisfaction from everything it attaches to. Addicted to their dependence on anger to remove obstacles to desire, they are driven to self-destruction by following its dictates. Addicted to delusion and confusion, they constantly reinforce their sense of alienation by piling theories upon misperceptions, getting themselves more confused, more fanatical, more removed from their own common sense.

Just like the wardens in the hells
And the forest of razor-sharp leaves,
This pain is produced by my own evolution,
With whom should I be angry?

Infinite consequences for thoughts, words, and acts lead in a positive direction to the highest heavens and divine embodiments as well as to perfect buddhahood. They lead in a negative direction to the extreme states of alienation, stress, and pain in the hells, the pretan ghost worlds, and the animal kingdoms. Should we find ourselves in a hell realm, being tortured by demons, would we bother to be angry with them for doing what is natural for them? Are we angry with fire for burning? They are merely the creations of our own negative actions in previous existences. We should be angry only with our own negative evolutionary actions.

Compelled by my evolutionary actions
Others come forth to harm me,
When that sends them to hell,
Have I not caused their downfall?

On top of that, we can take responsibility for these demons who now torment us, since they hurt us as a blind, involuntary reaction to our having hurt them in the past, our driving them into more and more vicious and harmful embodiments and environments. So we not only are not to be angry with them, we should feel remorse that we affected them so negatively in the past, which conditioned their ending up in such a state as their present one. Here we begin to enter the land of patience as active forgiveness. Joyfully, ecstatically, we celebrate our initial freedom from fear of suffering by going beyond patience as endurance and as forbearance and enter patience as nonretaliation and forgiveness. This is the antechamber of the temple of compassion.

> Relying on them with patience,
> Do I not purge myself of many sins?
> Yet when they relate to me with harm,
> Do they not suffer long the pains of hell?

Our enemies provide us with irritation, injury, and harm, which are the occasions for us to practice endurance, forbearance, and forgiveness. The worse they treat us the more we benefit. We are even harming them by allowing them to mistreat us, for they intend us harm, and the fruit of that intention and their harmful acts are a miserable future for them. We become stronger bodhisattva saviors, eventually buddhas, while they have long sessions undergoing hellish torments, which they don't benefit from since they have no idea about using suffering to practice patience.

> Since thus I injure them,
> And thus they benefit me,
> Why so perversely, savage mind,
> Do you feel anger toward them?

It is not yet time to go further into the interpersonal consideration about how not to harm others in this way by being overly patient and continuing to allow them to harm us. At this point, we still need to go deeper into our own situations and further reinforce our patience by minding again how much overkill it is to get angry with these poor enemies who are so effectively destroying themselves by harming us.

> If I have the excellence of patience,
> I'll never get close to any hell!
> Though I protect myself this way,
> How will it be for them?

Patience would make it impossible to be in hell, since the patient person would have used the suffering of all the preceding states to develop freedom and transcendence of suffering.

Patience is the ultimate armor against the onslaught of addiction and suffering.

> Yet if I retaliate by harming them,
> That will not serve to protect them,
> My own conduct will be destroyed,
> And all my discipline will be for nothing.

It might occur to us that what we should do to help out these poor enemies is to harm them back, thus giving them a chance to practice patience. This rationalization is tempting, since it could support our giving vent to our old habitual desire for righteous retaliation. But we quickly realize that harm and suffering only make the ordinary person angry, which makes them do all sorts of worse things, making their evolutionary downward momentum even greater. Once we start harming them and losing our control to anger on the way, we will lose our discipline as well, and fall back from our rise toward transcendence through progress in patience.

> My mind is not itself embodied,
> So no one can conquer it in any way;
> But its deep attachment to the body,
> Lets it be harmed by sufferings of the body.

This is a startling claim. Shantideva seems to refer to what the Buddhist Tantrics call the extremely subtle mind, with its virtual embodiment made of subtle energy, which is "not embodied" in, in the sense of not reducible to, the gross body that suffers pain so sensitively. You remind yourself here, as you are working on harm and anger and developing patience, that so much harm comes to you in your gross body and to your personality that identifies with it as you, and so is called your gross mind tied in with the six consciousnesses. Evolution holds your mind by holding your body hostage, getting to your mind by tormenting your body, and so making your mind angry, plunging it back into the anger addiction. This disembodied mind is esoterically the life-to-life-going selfless continuum that can be called your "relative soul," from the Buddhist relationalist perspective. By "not embodied," Shantideva does not mean that mind is some absolutely different thing from the body—the mind is always embodied, actually, whether in gross flesh and bone or subtle energy embodiment. He means only that it is not indivisibly committed to this one gross body, but will continue on to body after body in its evolutionary progress or retrogress. We need to remind ourselves in some such way of our ability to dis-identify from our gross bodies in order to develop the deepest, death- and pain-defying level of patience and immunity to anger.

Then we turn to our more subtle identities, on the level of speech and mind.

> But since contempt,
> Harsh words, and disrepute
> Can never injure the body,
> Why, mind, do you get so angry?

When we are harmed on the verbal level, the pain is not physical. Still it can be a powerful cause of anger—we often take strong offense, become highly indignant at insult, slander, abusive speech, and so on. Yet speech is just like an echo: it does not inflict real pain, not touching the body except when we let it arouse us.

> "Because others will dislike me!"
> But that will not consume me
> Either in this life or the next;
> So why should I dislike it?

We don't want others to think badly of us? Then don't get angry with the insults or bad talk of others. If we laugh and ignore attempts to provoke us, people will like us, not dislike us.

"Because it will block my worldly gain!"
Even if I don't like that,
I will leave my profits behind me here,
While I will continue riding on my sins.

Perhaps we think that we will suffer loss of reputation and thereby loss of income, if we ignore negative speech about us. But still that is no cause for anger, we should not be living for money. Besides, being angry will not restore our income and will often make our situation worse—we can think of better ways to defend our reputations and livelihood by staying cool and reasoning strategically.

Better that I die right now,
Worse that I live long by evil deeds;
Though I might hang on for quite a while,
Reality comes out in the suffering of death.

This may be going beyond where we want to go, in case we are either a secularist or even if we are religious formally but with our reality-view strongly tinged by secularism. It is hard for us, if we think we have only this life to live, that the causal chain of consequences stops cold at death, to live with a sense of responsibility for the results of our thoughts, words, and deeds that will emerge beyond this life. Even with ourselves out of the picture, we can sometimes think of the impact on posterity, our children, grandchildren, the planet, all beings, but it is difficult to make heavy sacrifice now for such a vague future result. To really go far enough inside to conquer the deep mental and emotional habit and even instinct of anger, it may be essential to be able to self-identify as a life continuum that includes a subtle energy self, detachable from the body of this life (sort of like identifying with our genes but making it more personal), to feel that the evolutionary causal chain in which our present thoughts, words, and deeds play a part will carry on involving us beyond our separation from our present gross bodymind complex. To be willing to die before getting carried away by anger, for example, may be necessary for the ultimate conquest of anger. With these thoughts, Shantideva moves us in that direction.

You dream of happiness for a hundred years,
And then you wake up.
You dream of happiness for an instant,
And then you wake up.

In both these wakenings
The happiness will not return;

Whether life is long or short,
Just like that, at death it ends the same.

Even if I gain great good fortune
And enjoy happiness for a long time,
At death I go on destitute with empty hands,
Just as if robbed by a thief.

Why should you think, speak, or act badly for a present gain in the present life in such a way that the long future will be experienced as horrible and ruinous for your happiness? Though it may seem to you now that you will be here for a very long time and so the goals you aim for have supreme importance, they are like goals in a dream, in an important sense. You could die at any moment—*you will die at some moment*—and all you will have gained in terms of profit, fame, and pleasure will instantly be lost to you. Yet you will continue as a being structured according to the patterns of habit and instinct you have formed through your thoughts, words, and deeds, the structuring coming, cumulatively of course, from an infinite past but significantly affected by your evolutionary acts in this present life. When this becomes common sense to you, you have a strong motive to shape your mental, verbal, and physical actions as consciously, positively, and beautifully as you can. You live this life like someone who does not spend his entire day in a warm bath, but rather goes out and sweats and trains in order to develop a beautiful and powerful body. Of course, you do take a nice hot shower afterward, so it is not total deferral of all gratification, just that your orientation is more complex than when you only aim at your immediate result.

It is highly important to complicate your orientation by expanding your horizon beyond your death that ends this life, when you seek victory in the struggle against anger. Or, it may be that you must remain inalterably convinced about either your nihilistic secularism or your absolutistic theism, firmly expecting either utter cessation of conscious existence or radically discontinuous fixed heavenly consciousness awarded by absolute God due to religious belief—no matter what your chain of actions. In those cases, the task is to invest enough concern in your impact on others, posterity, or community, that you can live here and now, enough beyond your self-concern in this life that your energy to restrain your anger becomes more powerful than your concern for your immediate goals.

"If I live and have good fortune,
I can wipe out sin and save up merit."
But if I use anger to attain that fortune,
Do I not consume all merit and accomplish sin?

If I am destroying the very merit
For the sake of which I am alive,
What is the use of living,
When all I do is intensify my sins?

You might think, "Well, I can use anger now to destroy this enemy, thereby prolonging and enriching my life and using it and its leisure to develop virtues such as patience." But then, the longer and richer life has already been given over to slavery under anger, and it will not be recovered easily for the cultivation of patience.

"I should be angry when people criticize me,
Since they thereby ruin others' confidence."
Then why don't you also get angry
When they criticize others?

"I can patiently tolerate such hostility,
Because it is aimed at another person!"
Then why can't I tolerate criticism of myself,
Since it aims only at my mentally addictive habits?

You don't mind criticism when you can dissociate its target from yourself, as when someone else is criticized and you feel perfectly fine about it. But when you are criticized, it is always because you have been greedy, angry, proud, stingy, prejudiced, or deluded, so it is these root mental addictions that are actually being criticized. When you get angry, it is because you are confused and identify yourself with your addictions.

> Should people slander or even destroy,
> Icons, sacred monuments or scriptures,
> My anger would be inappropriate,
> Since buddhas and so on cannot be injured.

We should not engage in religious absolutism and become angry and vengeful even if people commit sacrilege and destroy sacred objects. Enlightened beings are not the icons people make of them, and they are not concerned if material images or books or monuments are damaged. If they are not angry about it, why should you be? Journalists were surprised at me when I could not agree with those Buddhists who were outraged at the Taliban destruction of the great buddhas carved in the cliff sides at Bamiyan. Of course, Buddhists do believe that it is a negative evolutionary action to destroy a representation of something as positive as a buddha—it is harmful to the destroyer, who thereby deepens his alienation from his own potential of becoming free and enlightened some day. Thus they have already hurt themselves enough through their own destructive acts; it is unnecessary to become angry with them on top of that.

> I should stop my anger toward people
> Who harm mentors, relatives, and friends,
> Seeing as in the above cases
> How it arises from mechanical conditions.

> Since sensitive beings are injured
> Both by inanimate things and other beings,
> Why should I be angry only with the beings?
> Rather I should patiently tolerate all harm!

In these two cases you employ the patience of insight into relativity cultivated above.

> Should one person commit harm out of delusion,
> And another get angry out of delusion,
> Which one is to be more blamed?
> Which one is to be blameless?

Clearly delusion is to be blamed in both cases, the harmer and yourself who gets impatient and angry with it are both deluded about the reality of things, not realizing the evolutionary harmfulness of anger is just as great as causing an actual injury.

Why did I previously commit bad actions
Which now cause others to do me harm?
Since everything comes from my own past actions,
Why should I be angry with my enemies?

You are thinking of yourself as innocent and unreasonably attacked by your enemy, therefore your deluded anger is not as bad as his deluded harmfulness. However, the deeper cause of his harmfulness toward you is your harmful actions and anger toward him in previous existences. This levels the field, and the only way to break the beginningless vicious circle is to shun anger and exert your forbearance. Here again we make the immediate moment and its reaction and nonreaction infinite in significance by linking it to the infinite context of continuous relativity of life.

When I have understood this,
I should mindfully create merit,
Using every way to turn everyone
Toward mutually loving attitudes.

When the foundation of mindfulness has been laid, you can move farther in the positive direction of active compassion and love. Again, the multilife continuum of cause and effect is invoked to rise to the present occasion with sufficient force of patience.

Is a man condemned to die not lucky
When freed after only having his hand cut off?
Why am I who suffer human misery not lucky
When through it I am spared the pains of hell?

If I am hardly able to endure
The trivial pains of the here and now,
Since it's the source of hellish suffering,
Why do I not restrain my anger?

In order to satisfy my desires
I have already burned in countless hells,
By which bad evolution I did not fulfill
Any useful purpose for myself or others.

But now since a huge purpose is accomplished
By bearing harm which is tiny compared to hell,
I should really be ecstatically joyful
About a suffering which gets rid of harm for all!

Here we border on what might seem the masochistic, reveling in any suffering by totally experiencing it as sacrificial and expiative. (Here is where Jesus' passion is completely misunderstood if it is presented as a series of atrocities. Jesus, a transcendent hero who does not identify himself exclusively with his fleshly body, experiences the abuse heaped upon him by the Romans as ecstatic pain, in that he is using those pains to invite all sufferings of all beings upon himself, with his vow to expiate all of their sins by means of his self-sacrifice.)

If others take pleasure in praising
An excellent person (who is my rival),
Why don't you, oh my mind,
Be happy and also praise him?

Such joyful congratulatory happiness
Is not proscribed, but strongly recommended,
Widely taught by the Blissful Lords
And one of the supreme social virtues.

Congratulatory rejoicing is the supreme antidote to envy. One of my more humorous Lamas once said that it is the lazy person's way to accumulate merit and so progress toward buddhahood. They do something great with great effort and so gain merit. You refrain from envy at their accomplishment and merit, and you also get merit, a free ride, so to speak. (By the same token, you must be careful not to let your mind naughtily indulge in a perverse satisfaction over someone else's bad deed, since then you get a share of the sin or evolutionary demerit!)

When my excellence is discussed,

I want others to be happy too;

But when others' excellence is the topic,

I don't want even myself to be happy.

You lose doubly when your rival is praised, if you let your mind go with envy. Not only did you not get the praise or the success, on top of that your disgruntlement makes you more unhappy.

Since I conceived the spirit of enlightenment

By wanting all beings to find happiness,

Why do I become angry

When they find happiness on their own?

Your rival is among the "all sensitive beings" whom you vow to free from suffering. Here they have gotten a bit of relative happiness due to a little success without your making any effort at all, and yet you are unhappy. What did your vow then mean?

If I don't like others to get any good,

Where is my spirit of enlightenment?

How could I have that spirit

If I get angry about others' fortune?

Praise and so on are but distractions,
They destroy my disillusion with cyclic life,
They stir my rivalry with the excellent,
And destroy my chance of real success.

Praise and fame can become addictive and distract us from pursuing what is truly meaningful in our lives. Seeming to be an advantage, they deflect our attention from the real aim of life, which is evolutionary development toward perfect buddhahood.

Thus those who aim to destroy
My reputation and so on,
Are they not also deeply engaged
In preventing my fall to the lower depths?

Those who seek to backbite us and destroy our reputation by lying about us or exaggerating our negative qualities are actually helping us to avoid distractions and stick to the main focus of life.

Dedicated to achieving liberation,
I don't need bonds of gain and status,
When one frees me from my bonds,
How can I resent him?

So, we should gleefully appreciate those who strain themselves to harm us verbally by turning others against us.

> Those who want me to suffer
> Are like buddhas blessing me,
> They elevate me beyond all dangers;
> Why should I resent them?

Here we entertain the supreme patience, going beyond "forgive them for they know not what they do!" to "Thank them for they catapult me toward supreme felicity!"—at great karmic cost to themselves, negative evolutionary patterning that they attain by causing harm.

> "But if he obstructs my gaining merit?"
> It's not right to be angry with him even then,
> For there is no discipline as good as patience,
> And doesn't he help me abide in it?

> If I, by my own shortcomings,
> Fail to remain patient with him,
> I have finally only obstructed myself
> From using this occasion for merit.

> If one thing won't happen without another,

And if it does happen when it's there,
That other thing is the cause of the one;
How can it become its obstructor?

When I make a gift, the recipient
Will not obstruct my generosity.
The bestowers of monastic graduation,
Do not obstruct monastic graduation.

There are plenty of recipients in this world,
But the one who causes harm is rare;
If I don't cause them harm,
Beings usually won't harm me.

Therefore, I should rejoice in my enemy;
He helps my practice of enlightenment,
Being just like a treasure found at home
Without having to go out and get it.

My most humorous and creative Lama, the late Tara Tulku, really shocked me. I had already been practicing Buddhism for years and thinking myself to have made some progress, when he said if I really knew what I was doing here, I would be happier to come down for breakfast in the morning to meet my worst enemy than I would be to greet a TV prize show host ringing my doorbell and presenting me with a check for $10 million. I had to admit to myself I was still far, far from this attainment. Even now, it seems impossible, and all my excuses won't really bring me up to the impact of this verse. Of course, I could perhaps use the $10 million treasure to accomplish much generous giving and teaching, and the worst enemy might be happier if I helped him or her, even with some ferocity, overcome that habit of enmity. The point here is I should be able to treasure the enemy, able to use the harm to develop transcendent patience, since there are perhaps more recipients of my gifts than there are enemies to give me the patience opportunities that are injuries.

> I can practice patience with him;
> So he deserves my first offering
> Of the fruits of patience to him,
> Since he is the cause of patience.

The Dalai Lama's long decades of meditation on Mao, the great enemy of Tibet, its leader, and its people, is the perfect example of this. When asked once at Asia Society about whom he most admired in the world, he mentioned not only Gandhi, the apostle of nonviolence, but also Mao, an apostle of violence and the destroyer of Tibetan freedom, its Dharma institutions, its environment, and over a million of its people. Was this admiration going too far, a carryover from the Dalai Lama's meditation of appreciating his enemy? Was it showing still a trace of selfishness, focusing on the patience development he could extract from this harm, rather than on the need to save Mao himself from the negative effects of causing the harm and his Tibetan people from the destructive effects of the harm?

> "But that enemy does not deserve such veneration,
> Since he doesn't want me to practice patience."
> Then why venerate the Holy Dharma,
> Since it too is but a cause for practice.

This is the deep depths of the obstruction to forgiveness. We note the evil intention of the enemy, that he wants to cause us harm, he is a malicious agency of harm, so why should we not only forgive him but also appreciate him, adding transcendent love to transcendent patience? He is just an evil enemy, we should destroy him, says our angry mind! But we answer ourselves, "Well we appreciate and love the teaching, the Dharma, though it is impersonal and has no intention to help us. Our enemy is just our opportunity to practice this most rare and important transcendent virtue."

"But this enemy is not to be venerated
Since he does intend to harm me!"
How could I ever practice patience,
If everyone tried like my doctor just to help me?

Thus since patience is developed
Relying on those with hate in their hearts,
They are as fit for veneration as the Holy Dharma,
Since both are causes of patience.

Here is the true buddha-mind, the equality wisdom, seeing the equality between a hate-filled mind and the Holy Dharma! Here is the patient tolerance of the intolerant. Here is love returned for hate, good for evil. This is the realm of all the great spiritual persons and deities of the past.

The following verses are a song of celebration for Buddha, Jesus, Moses, Muhammad, Mencius, Laotzu, and every saint and adept from every spiritual tradition throughout history, along with the many unsung mothers, wives, and working women throughout all societies who put up with so much abuse and injury and still persist in making peace, creating harmony, opening the door to joy in spite of all the miserable situations brought upon them by all the foolishness and violence of men.

Therefore the Muni Buddha said
The world of beings is the buddhaverse;
The many who have satisfied those beings
Have thereby attained transcendence.

The "buddhaverse" is the universe in its deepest reality as experienced by enlightened beings, no longer a "universe" turning around one self-centered being, themselves, or some projection of their isolated self as being an absolute omnipotent and unaffected deity. This buddhaverse, "pure land," enlightenment mandala is nothing but the interactive mindfield of sensitive beings, including gods, demons, hell-beings, animals, ghosts, and so forth. A bodhisattva thus creates a buddhafield by serving and making those beings happy. Thus, an infinite vicious cycle of enmity and injury is ended, and the buddhaversal beauty of patience is built when the bodhisattva does not react to injury, but embraces the harming person with patience, love, acceptance, forgiveness, and even appreciation.

Beings and buddhas are alike
As both cause gain of buddha-qualities;
As I adore the buddhas,
There is no way not to adore beings.

Further, since buddhas are beings' true friends,
Who accomplish their measureless benefits,
What other way is there to repay such kindness
Than to love and satisfy those beings?

Buddhas have given their bodies and entered hells for beings,
So gratitude to buddhas means helping those same beings;
Thus even if beings cause the greatest harm,
I must treat all with most resourceful goodness.

Did not Jesus join the Buddha when he said that those who see me in the least of these truly see me?

When beings are happy, buddhas are pleased,
When they are harmed, buddhas are harmed.
I will love them and delight the buddhas;
For if I hurt them, I will hurt the buddhas.

Just as the senses can find no pleasure
When the body is ablaze with flames,
So when beings are being harmed
There is no way to delight the Compassionate.

Thus since I have harmed these beings,
And caused displeasure to the Compassionate,

I now repent and confess these sins,
And beg your indulgence for such displeasure.

In order to please the Transcendent Lords,
From now on I will control myself and serve the world,
Let the many beings kick me, trample my head, or kill me—
May the World-Saviors rejoice as I will not retaliate.

Why don't I see that every good thing comes
From pleasing sensitive beings,
Not only my future gain of buddhahood,
But also glory, fame, and happiness in this very life?

Even in the normal life cycle, patience bestows
Beauty, health, and fame,
And supports a nice long life,
And the joy of a universal monarch.

CHAPTER TEN

Resigning to Anger
—The Ultimate Level

First let me be clear that this time, resigning to anger never means giving way to anger again. Rather, it means recovering the powerful energy previously controlled by anger, the energy of fire, combustion, illumination that dispels all shadows, and wielding it with wisdom.

When patience has gone as far as it can go, and the enlightened person has become transcendent through it, there is no more need to use injury as an opportunity to develop more. None of the transcendences can be fully achieved without all of them being fully achieved. Patience transcends when wisdom transcends, when selflessness is fully experienced, and there is no more any real difference between enemy, injurer, injury, and injured patient. The transcendently patient cannot be injured because transcendent patience has filled her with inviolate and inexhaustible bliss. Her bliss of supreme union remains aware of apparent individuation, but is never marred, even by her ongoing compassionate sensitivity to the still-apparent suffering of any other part of her infinitely selfless body that encompasses all living beings. She understands how their suffering still overwhelms them due to their erroneous sense of alienation from others, which causes them to close off the reality of their own potential bliss. In their pain, they seek to break through their isolation by injuring others, including her, but the apparent injury cannot disturb her bliss.

Once anger is conquered by the yogas of tolerance, insight, and forgiveness patience, its furious fire is still there to be used creatively by the heroic angel of wisdom. Anger now becomes creativity transcendence; anger becomes joyous heroic energy.

At this point, the choice of interaction with those who are relatively separate and relatively suffering is no longer obstructed by the need to extract one's own further development from the situation. There is no further evolutionary self-interest involved, not because one has become a self-effacing martyr, but because one has become a self-fulfilled, ecstatic, blissful, perfectly self-satisfied being, a "bliss-void-indivisible" person—sometimes also called a "Heruka"—the kind of heroine or hero that embodies selflessness with compassion.

Here in this realm, the energy wielded so destructively by anger becomes free for creative use. To quote again the late great Tara Tulku, these energies were all to be destroyed by wisdom when they were constituting a world of suffering based on ignorance. Delusion, pride/stinginess, lust/greed, envy, and finally anger—all are to be destroyed. Delusion is ignorance or misknowledge and is the root of all of them, since they all depend on the reification of the self-other distinction, the absolutization of the self of subjects and objects, persons and things. When misknowledge is finally destroyed, the energies become the energies of freedom. Wisdom can reappropriate them and use them to rebuild a world of freedom and bliss.

Delusion becomes the mirror wisdom, revealing the world of material forms to be a mirror of relativity, of diamond white freedom, of each seemingly self-subsistent material thing's self-transcendence into pure interrelationship. Pride/stinginess becomes the equality wisdom, insightfully aware of the equality of self and other, person and thing, the golden yellow radiance of pure generosity, as all beings and things give themselves to all others. Lust/greed becomes the individuating wisdom, the ruby red energy wherein compassion blissfully and artfully creates beautiful forms to interact with alienated suffering beings to embrace them in nurturing, releasing, liberating relationship with all other beings and things. Envy/rivalry becomes the emerald green energy that unifies self and other into inconceivably powerful combinations that can accomplish what seem like wonders to ordinary alienated, isolated beings.

Finally, anger's explosive energy becomes the bright blue-black sapphire radiant laser light of absolute purity wisdom, the completely inexorable, relatively absolute energy that absorbs all differences and oppositions, that destroys all obstructions, dissects all complexities and knots of resistance to freedom, that consumes death and life and all between in the infinitely free. It is so powerful in its destruction of all egotism and confusion it cannot be opposed. It is freedom itself, it is freedom that is free of freedom even, free of being free, and so is infinitely present in every level of sensitive and creative relationship. It is like an atom bomb, a hydrogen explosion, a black hole and a pulsar, a lightning and a diamond, revealing the supreme reality of nonduality, absolute relative unity, self and other communion, wisdom and compassion, bliss void indivisible.

The fierce buddha-embodiments illustrate this most powerful energy. Yamantaka ("Death-Exterminator") or Vajrabhairava ("Diamond Terrifier") are contemplative Buddha forms that serve as the supreme icons of the Anger at Anger. The buddha-continuing-as-bodhisattva, Manjushri, the eternal youth of transcendent wisdom, manifests this exquisite, terrible embodiment of wisdom's immortality. Though we will tremble with fear when we encounter this, we need only to remember, when even Death is terminated, then there is no more death, even for Death, and Death becomes one with Infinite Life.

Bibliography

Aristotle. *Rhetoric*. Translated by W. Rhys Roberts. Franklin Center, PA: Franklin Library Edition, 1981.

Chaucer, Geoffrey. *The Canterbury Tales*. Translated by J. U. Nicolson. Franklin Center, PA: Franklin Library Edition, 1981.

Plutarch. *Moralia*. Translated by W. C. Helmbold. Cambridge: Harvard University Press, 1984.

Schimmel, Solomon. *The Seven Deadly Sins: Jewish, Christian, and Classical Reflections on Human Psychology*. New York: Oxford University Press, 1997.

Seneca. *Moral and Political Essays*. Edited and translated by J. M. Cooper and J. F. Procopé. New York: Cambridge University Press, 1995.

Shantideva. *Introduction to the Way of Enlightenment*. Translated by Robert A. F. Thurman. *Essential Tibetan Buddhism*. San Francisco: Harper-Collins, 1999.

Index